The Wireshark Field Guide

The Wireshark Field Guide
Analyzing and Troubleshooting Network Traffic

Robert Shimonski

ELSEVIER

AMSTERDAM • BOSTON • HEIDELBERG • LONDON
NEW YORK • OXFORD • PARIS • SAN DIEGO
SAN FRANCISCO • SINGAPORE • SYDNEY • TOKYO
Syngress is an imprint of Elsevier

SYNGRESS.

Acquiring Editor: Chris Katsaropoulos
Development Editor: Benjamin Rearick
Project Manager: Mohana Natarajan

Syngress is an imprint of Elsevier
225 Wyman Street, Waltham, MA 02451, USA

First published 2013

Notices
Knowledge and best practice in this field are constantly changing. As new research and experience broaden our understanding, changes in research methods, professional practices, or medical treatment may become necessary.

Practitioners and researchers must always rely on their own experience and knowledge in evaluating and using any information, methods, compounds, or experiments described herein. In using such information or methods they should be mindful of their own safety and the safety of others, including parties for whom they have a professional responsibility.

To the fullest extent of the law, neither the Publisher nor the authors, contributors, or editors, assume any liability for any injury and/or damage to persons or property as a matter of products liability, negligence or otherwise, or from any use or operation of any methods, products, instructions, or ideas contained in the material herein.

British Library Cataloguing in Publication Data
A catalogue record for this book is available from the British Library

Library of Congress Cataloging-in-Publication Data
A catalog record for this book is available from the Library of Congress

ISBN: 978-0-12-410413-6

For information on all Syngress publications
visit our website at **www.syngress.com**

This book has been manufactured using Print On Demand technology. Each copy is produced to order and is limited to black ink. The online version of this book will show color figures where appropriate.

DEDICATION

This book is dedicated to my wonderful children, Dylan Shimonski and Vienna Shimonski. I love you!

CONTENTS

Welcome to *The Wireshark Field Guide: Analyzing and Troubleshooting Network Traffic* book, your guide to get up to speed using Wireshark in a quick and efficient manner. This book provides hackers, pen testers, and network administrators with practical guidance on capturing and interactively browsing the traffic running on a computer network. Wireshark is the world's foremost network protocol analyzer, with a rich feature set that includes deep inspection of hundreds of protocols, live capture, offline analysis, and many other features.

Wireshark is a multiplatform application that can be set up and put to work in minutes to help analyze and troubleshoot some of the most complex security problems found today. This book covers the installation, configuration, and use of this powerful tool. It provides readers with the hands-on skills to be more productive with Wireshark as they drill down into the information contained in real-time network traffic.

- Learn the fundamentals of using Wireshark in a concise field manual.
- Quickly create functional filters that will allow you to get to work quickly on solving problems.
- Understand the myriad of options and the deep functionality of Wireshark to get working quicker.
- Solve common problems seen in networks today with what is taught in this guide.
- Learn some advanced features, methods, and helpful ways to work quicker and more efficient.

The goal of this book is to teach the basics quickly in a very short format publication. Use the following link and similar other links found at the books companion website www.learnwireshark.com.

ABOUT THE AUTHOR

Robert Shimonski (www.shimonski.com) is a best-selling author and editor with over 15 years experience developing, producing, and distributing print media in the form of books, magazines, and periodicals. To date, Rob has successfully created over 100 books that are currently in circulation. Rob has worked for countless companies including CompTIA, Entrepreneur Magazine, Microsoft, McGraw-Hill Education, Cisco, the National Security Agency, and Digidesign.

Rob also has over 15 years experience in direct support of network infrastructures and systems and has spent a considerable amount of that time in leading teams in operational support and engineering architecture. Rob authored the award-winning Syngress book *Sniffer Pro Network Optimization and Troubleshooting Handbook* back in 2002. He has also contributed to many other network and security-related publications on penetration, security design, network analysis, and systems engineering. He can be reached online at www.shimonski.com or at www.learnwireshark.com.

ACKNOWLEDGMENT

I would like to thank all who made this book possible. Special thanks to Pete Cheung for his technical help in creating this book and to Chris and Ben for their assistance in producing this book.

INTRODUCTION

Welcome to the Syngress "Wireshark Field Guide," your indispensable companion to using Wireshark successfully and solving problems with one of the most commonly used tools in the networking arena today. In this concise text, I will cover how to acquire Wireshark, what you need to know about it to get it up and running and then using it to help solve problems.

For over two decades, the need for an understanding of protocol analysis has grown as the networks we rely on to connect our computers, mobile devices, and systems to use the Internet, access the cloud, and work within our corporate networks have also grown. As more reliance on using the network becomes the norm, solving problems quickly is also becoming increasingly more important.

As we will learn in this book, Wireshark (as well as other protocol analysis tools) is used often to help find and solve problems on internetworks for all sizes. In this book, we will cover the following sections:

ABOUT WIRESHARK

Experienced network technicians, operators, and engineers across the globe use Wireshark and tools of its kind to solve problems and we will cover not only the nuts and bolts of using it but also why we do. In this section, we will briefly go over the history of Wireshark as well as to discuss the use of packet capture and analysis in the field of networking. First, we need to understand the history of Wireshark and packet capture and analysis to get a solid understanding of the purpose of using this tool. An in-depth look at Wireshark, its features, and the toolset are covered as well as a granular look at the specifics of why protocol capture and analysis is so critical to solving problems.

INSTALLING WIRESHARK

In this chapter of the book, we will cover how to get Wireshark, install it, and set it up for use on a computer. We will cover how the tool changes your network interface card (NIC) so that it can capture data, specifically what requirements would be needed in order to not only install but also use Wireshark in production as well as many other tidbits of information to make your troubleshooting time painless and productive. We will briefly go over the interface and how to launch and use the tool.

CONFIGURING A SYSTEM

Once your computer is ready to go, you will need to learn how to use Wireshark on a network. This is not a simple task because there are specific configuration changes you will need to make not only on your computer system but also components on the network in order to capture and analyze data. In this chapter, we will cover not only configuration of network devices but also teach you how to consider the specific placement of the tool in order to use it correctly. We will learn how preparing to capture data may require making adjustments on network devices, network cabling, or configuration specifics necessary to capture data. We will learn how to configure a network device to send data to Wireshark, the correct placement and staging of the capture device(s) as well as the strategy you must plan with two end-to-end systems when more than one Wireshark capture is needed.

CAPTURING PACKETS

In this chapter, we will learn the art of capturing packets in order to decode them, analyze them, and inspect what is traversing your network. Once you have started to capture packets, the rest of the chapters leading up to the last chapter (saving captures and saving files) you will be learning about the interface and how to manipulate it to troubleshoot problems. This chapter covers the three panes and all details within them, running captures, how to start and stop Wireshark as well as be given a sample problem to work with.

COLOR CODES

Deeper inspection within the capture is required. In this chapter, we will learn how Wireshark color codes the captures and how to quickly look for problems. In this chapter, we will also learn more about protocols, ports, and other critical network-based information that will help you solve problems.

FILTERS

How to filter captures correctly is the key to finding problems especially when running Wireshark on networks where a lot of data traverses. Consider capturing data from one system communicating with another ... what would you specifically search for to help solve a problem? Filtering on protocols, IP addresses and using specific Boolean arguments commonly used today are covered as well as specific example of filters that you can use right away to help get you up and running with Wireshark immediately.

SAMPLE CAPTURES

In this chapter, we will expand on what we learned in the Filters chapter by covering some advanced problems, how to solve them using Wireshark, and the more complex use of analysis by applying more filters and reviewing expert analysis reports.

INSPECTING PACKETS

As we learn more about Wireshark, we will discuss problems found on a network and specifically why they occur from the packet level. In this chapter, we will take an in-depth look at a few common (and not so common) problems and what you are looking for in the packets, how to use the tool to get and view this information, and how to use Wireshark to solve them. We will also look at other tools you can use to augment the use of Wireshark to solve complex network and system issues.

DEEP ANALYSIS

In this chapter, we take a deeper look into the packets in order to define and find root cause of problems as well as how to use Wireshark and other enterprise tools to solve problems that occur over wide area network links. We will learn about probes, taps, and how all of these tools can be used together to create a complete picture to help you not only understand why data traverses a network a certain way but also why it chooses specific paths, how it interacts with destination systems, and what could go wrong within those conversations. We will look at voice over IP (VoIP) problems, malicious software issues, how intrusion detection/prevention, scanning, and many other services work on a network and how Wireshark can help you work with them when solving issues.

SAVING CAPTURES

Once you are completed with your analysis, you may want to save and archive your files for future use. This chapter covers file formats, how to use capture files with other protocol analysis systems, how to generate reports and more.

Now, let us get our hands dirty and starting inspecting data to solve problems!

About Wireshark

1.1 INTRODUCTION

Experienced network technicians, operators, and engineers across the globe use Wireshark and tools of its kind to solve problems and we will cover the how and why. In this section, we will briefly go over the history of Wireshark as well as to discuss the use of packet capture and analysis in the field of networking. First, we need to understand the history of Wireshark and packet capture, and analysis to get a solid understanding of the purpose of using this tool. Once we cover Wireshark's historical background, we will cover the most current release, how to get it and what you need to prepare for an install and setup of the product. We will also cover the fundamentals of packet capture and analysis so that you are aware of what the tool is inherently used for.

This book can be used by beginners and those new to networking, however, having a background and solid knowledge on the topic will make reading, understanding, and absorbing this book much easier.

1.2 WHAT IS WIRESHARK?

Protocol capture and analysis is nothing new, it is actually been around for decades. With the release of UNIX systems, many tools contained directly in the operating system allowed for the capture and review of packet level data for the purpose of solving problems. As data moves across a network from client to server or to printers, across wireless access points, and across the Internet, it moves in the form of electrical signals and frequencies. A packet capture tool (also called a network analyzer) can be used to capture this data for analysis. A network analyzer is a troubleshooting tool that is used to find and solve network communication problems, plan network capacity, and perform network optimization. Network analyzers can capture all the traffic that is going across your network and interpret the captured traffic to decode and interpret the different protocols in use. The decoded data is shown in a format that makes it easy to understand, peeling away the layers of encapsulated data that is used to identify it or enable it to be used on the network. A network analyzer can also capture only traffic that matches the selection criteria as defined by a filter. This allows a technician to capture only traffic that is relevant to the problem at hand. A typical network analyzer displays the decoded data in three panes:

- Summary: Displays a one-line summary of the highest layer protocol contained in the frame, as well as the time of the capture and the source and destination addresses.
- Detail: Provides details on all the layers inside the frame.
- Hex: Displays the raw captured data in hexadecimal format.

Figure 1.1 shows the Wireshark tool with captured data ready for inspection. In the figure, we can see all three panes in use. From top to bottom, you can see the Summary, Detail, and Hex panes. The Summary pane shows the high-level detail, such as sequence numbering of captured packets, the time captured, source and destination address, protocol used, length, and other information. If you select a packet in the summary pane, you can see more granular detail in the detail pane. By drilling down even further, you can select details in the Detail pane and see the specific hex data captured in the Hex pane.

As we work through this guide, we will dig deeper into each pane and learn exact specifics on how to use it, interpret what is in it, and troubleshoot problems. Network analyzers further provide the ability to create display filters so that a network professional can quickly find what he or she is looking for.

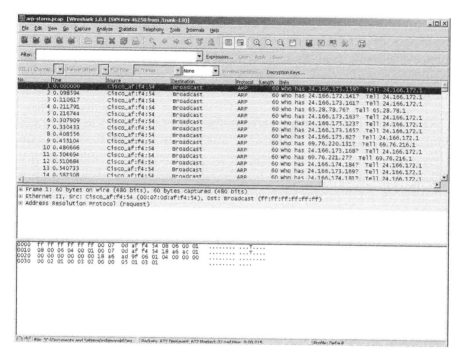

Figure 1.1 Using Wireshark.

Advanced network analyzers provide pattern analysis capabilities. This feature allows the network analyzer to go through thousands of packets and identify problems. The network analyzer can also provide possible causes for these problems and hints on how to resolve them.

1.3 WHAT IS NETWORK AND PROTOCOL ANALYSIS?

Electronic distribution of information is becoming increasingly important, and the complexity of the data exchanged between systems is increasing at a rapid pace. Computer networks today carry all kinds of data, voice, and video traffic. Network applications require full availability without interruption or congestion. As the information systems in a company grow and develop, more networking devices are deployed, resulting in large physical ranges covered by the networked system. It is crucial that this networked system operates as effectively as possible, because downtime is both costly and an inefficient use of available resources. Network and/or protocol analysis is a range of techniques that network engineers and technicians use to study the properties of networks, including connectivity, capacity, and performance. Network analysis can be used to estimate the capacity of an existing network, look at performance characteristics, or plan for future applications and upgrades.

One of the best tools for performing network analysis is a network analyzer like Wireshark. A network analyzer is a device that gives you a very good idea of what is happening on a network by allowing you to look at the actual data that travels over it, packet by packet. A typical network analyzer understands many protocols, which enables it to display conversations taking place between hosts on a network. Wireshark can be used in this capacity.

Network analyzers typically provide the following capabilities:

• Capture and decode data on a network
• Analyze network activity involving specific protocols
• Generate and display statistics about the network activity
• Perform pattern analysis of the network activity.

Packet capture and protocol decoding is sometimes referred to as "sniffing." This term came about because of the nature of the network analyzers ability to "sniff" traffic on the network and capture it.

Figures 1.1 and 1.2 show the Wireshark tool with captured data with a typical problem seen on network today—an address resolution protocol (ARP) storm. Figure 1.2 allows you to look deeper into the

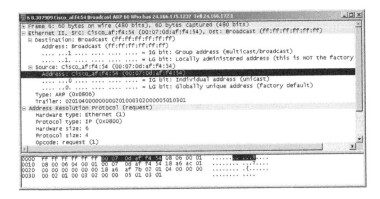

Figure 1.2 Performing protocol analysis.

data in order to troubleshoot the issue. Although we will get more involved in later chapters covering how to inspect traffic in detail, here you can see how a network analyzer performs "protocol analysis."

When decoding the capture of ARP packets, we can drill down into the tool (and the packets) to find the source and destination addresses of the storm. Now, Wireshark cannot solve all of your problems without some help! First, it takes you the technician with the inquisitive mind to first understand where to place Wireshark to capture this data. It then takes some inspect and analysis work to review what was captured and at minimum a basic understanding on how data works on a network. It also takes detective work on your part... you will need to know how to trace this ARP problem (in the form of a MAC address) to the offending client causing the storm. You will then need to know how to fix said problem. As you can see, protocol capture and analysis with a network analyzer tool like Wireshark only helps you begin to paint a picture of a problem, it does not always solve it directly for you.

●●●————————————————————————————

Beware of false positives. What this means is, you may see a problem, however, it is in fact not a problem but normal behavior. You may get a capture or a report from a network analyzer that may instruct you that a problem exists when it in fact does not. Using a network analyzer and performing network analysis is a function of a scientific mind. You not only need to question what you see but you may also need to conduct further testing and analysis to find root cause of a problem. Do not jump to conclusions, scientifically sort out the data, analyze and conduct research, discuss possibilities with peers and colleagues if you are not sure of your findings.

————————————————————————————

1.4 THE HISTORY OF WIRESHARK

Wireshark (http://www.wireshark.org/) is a software application used to capture and inspect protocol level data. As data traverses a network from clients to servers (as an example), the data is sent and although there are many tools of its kind, it is a tool that can be freely downloaded on the Internet. The history of Wireshark is one of many twists and turns. Although the tool has always been for the most part very reliable and incredibly useful, it has changed names and hands quite a few times.

One of the first well-known versions of Wireshark came in the form of Ethereal. Due to copyright issues and legal problems, the name was changed to Wireshark. We can, however, start this tools history back when it was named Ethereal. Ethereal (and its new form Wireshark) is an open-source freeware network analyzer available freely for download and can be used on many computer system platforms. In its infancy, tools such as Sniffer Pro were more robust and somewhat costly. Other tools like those sold by Fluke Networks were not only costly but also distributed with hardware raising its cost. Ethereal when released was not as robust and provided protocol decode features, however, lacked a number of features that the other tools available provided, such as the ability to monitor applications, expert analysis, advanced reporting tools, and the ability to capture mangled frames. Wireshark is the current version of the Ethereal tool, which now handles expert analysis and many of the other features that were missing from previous versions.

WinPcap (http://www.winpcap.org/) is the "other" application that must be used with Wireshark. WinPcap is nothing more than a library that Wireshark pulls from within a Windows system. Non-Windows based systems may use libcap. Either one used supplies a driver that allows for the capture of packets at the system and hardware level. We will learn in the next chapter that your network interface card (NIC) must be used in promiscuous mode in order to capture packets, and Wireshark uses these libraries to facilitate that functionality. When you download and use Wireshark, this set of libraries comes with it and must be installed with Wireshark in order to use it. This library set has been produced and distributed by a company named CACE (http://www.cacetech.com/).

A few years ago, CACE was purchased by a company named Riverbed (http://www.riverbed.com/), which is also a provider of network analysis and reporting tools, software, and hardware. With Riverbed behind CACE and supporting Wireshark, it is likely that this powerhouse trio of groups can not only bring network analysis to a new level but also give Wireshark more steam to grow into an even more robust application than it is today.

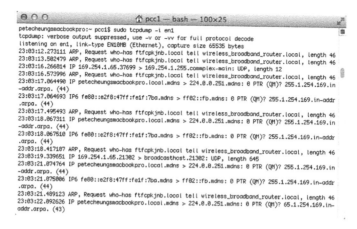

Figure 1.3 Using tcpdump.

Using tcpdump

Tcpdump (http://www.tcpdump.org/) is a protocol capture/packet analyzer that is used at the command line. Much like Wireshark [which uses a graphical user interface (GUI)], it captures packets and shows specific details about them which can be used for granular analysis of a problem. It also worked with libcap and puts the NIC in promiscuous mode allowing for the capturing of packets. It shows at the command line details and can be tailors with switches to show more or less specific detail. It is extremely helpful when you need to capture data at the time of problem as it is normally always installed and ready on most systems, primarily UNIX based. It is also freely available with the operating system you install.

Figure 1.3 shows the use of tcpdump on a UNIX system. Here we can view the conversations between two hosts, the one it is installed on (the source) and the destination address it is communicating with.

As you can see here, it is very easy to use and manipulate. You can get much of the same data out of tcpdump as you can with Wireshark, however, Wireshark will provide you with more bells and whistles, such as an easy to use GUI, an expert analysis tool, and reporting tools.

You can also find tcpdump on many of the UNIX-based firewalls deployed today. Firewalls, such as those from McAfee and Juniper, have tcpdump integrated into their toolsets so that they can be quickly invoked to solve or report on a problem.

●●●—————————————————————————————————

For those who use Windows based systems, you can download and install WinDump, which is the Windows version of tcpdump. Like tcpdump uses libcap, WinDump like Wireshark on Windows uses WinPcap. For Windows 7, Windows 8, and Server 2008 SP2, the "netsh trace start capture = yes" command is a good alternative to tcpdump. No installation is required to capture packets.

1.5 TROUBLESHOOTING PROBLEMS

Now that we have learned about protocol capture and analysis, and how Wireshark fits into the picture, let us continue to expand on its use by discussing how Wireshark can be used to analyze data. Although we will go into greater detail as we progress through this book, it is worthwhile to introduce the topic so we can begin to build on it.

When you work with a network or are directly responsible for it, you will often hear that there are problems with it. Some are common help desk requests from users who have problems remembering their system passwords, and others are calls from users who cannot login because their network cable got unplugged again. Although these are common problems, and annoying at times, they are easily fixed through a quick series of troubleshooting steps and usually require a simple solution.

Next on the complaint list are the calls from users who say that the network is too slow. That is a common complaint, but what happens when almost all the users on your network call en masse to complain about the speed of their logins, hanging applications, or timed out sessions? Obviously, there could be a problem with network performance if the majority of your users call to complain. Where do you begin to look for the source of this problem? With enterprise networks growing and connecting to other companies' networks increasingly rapidly, monitoring network performance can become a cumbersome task.

To investigate problems and attempt to find root cause you need to initially isolate a problem, monitor the network's performance using Wireshark, and then work to correct the issues. If performance is the issue, what are the many things we can look at in the map to troubleshoot where the problems are occurring and how to diagnose them correctly? Questions you need to ask immediately upon starting performance analysis are:

- Is poor network performance affecting one user, several users, or the entire network?

- Is the poor performance centered at a particular location or the entire network?
- When exactly did you start noticing poor performance or has it always been bad?
- Have any recent changes taken place—no matter how large or small?
- Are all applications at a particular location experiencing problems, or are problems localized to a specific application?
- Do you have any network documentation or topology maps?

These are but a sampling of the questions that could be asked but some of the most common. Ultimately, we will want to use Wireshark to troubleshoot and solve problems but it must be manipulated by someone such as yourself who knows how to uncover problems. Finding the root cause of a problem is what we can use this tool to accomplish at a granular level if your detective work is done correctly. You will want to capture data from the network, analyze it and use common network model, knowledge of protocols and specific methodology to assist in analyzing the problem and the data captured.

1.6 USING WIRESHARK TO ANALYZE DATA

The key to successful troubleshooting is knowing how the network functions under normal conditions. This knowledge allows a network engineer to quickly recognize abnormal operations. Using a strategy for network troubleshooting, the problem can be approached methodically and resolved with minimum disruption to customers. Unfortunately, many network professionals with years of experience have not mastered the basic concept of troubleshooting; a few minutes spent evaluating the symptoms can save hours of time lost chasing the wrong problem.

A good approach to problem resolution involves these steps:

- Recognizing symptoms and defining the problem
- Isolating and understanding the problem
- Identifying and testing the cause of the problem
- Solving the problem
- Verifying that the problem has been resolved
- If the problem is not found, reiterate until resolved or use to find more data to analyze.

The first step toward trying to solve a network issue is to recognize the symptoms. You might hear about a problem in one of many ways:

an end user might complain that he or she is experiencing performance or connectivity issues, or a network management station might notify you about it. Compare the problem to normal operation. Determine whether something was changed on the network just before the problem started. In addition, check to make sure you are not troubleshooting something that has never worked before. Write down a clear definition of the problem.

Once the problem has been confirmed and the symptoms identified, the next step is to isolate and understand the problem. When the symptoms occur, it is your responsibility to gather data for analysis and to narrow down the location of the problem. The best approach to reduce the problem's scope is to use divide-and-conquer methods. Try to figure out if the problem is related to a segment of the network or a single station. Determine if the problem can be duplicated elsewhere on the network.

The third step in problem resolution is to identify and test the cause of the problem. You can use network analyzers and other tools to analyze the traffic. After you develop a theory about the cause of the problem, you must test it.

Once a resolution to the problem has been determined, it should be put in place. The solution might involve upgrading hardware or software. It may call for increasing LAN segmentation or upgrading hardware to increase capacity.

The final step is to ensure that the entire problem has been resolved by having the end customer test for the problem. Sometimes a fix for one problem creates a new problem. At other times, the problem you repaired turns out to be a symptom of a deeper underlying problem. If the problem is indeed resolved, you should document the steps you took to resolve it. If, however, the problem still exists, the problem-solving process must be repeated from the beginning.

To understand network analysis, it is very important to learn the theory behind how networks operate. For a network to work, the computers running on it need to agree on a set of rules. Such a set of rules is known as a protocol. A protocol in networking terms is very similar to a language in human terms. Two computers using different protocols to talk to each other would be like someone trying to communicate in Japanese to another person who did not understand that language. It simply would not work!

Many protocols exist in today's world of network communication. In the early days of networking, each networking vendor wrote its own protocol. Eventually, standards were developed so that devices from multiple vendors could communicate with each other using a common protocol. The most commonly used protocol is the transmission control protocol/Internet protocol (TCP/IP).

We will cover the granular details of TCP/IP in later chapters when we begin digging into the packets we captured.

To use Wireshark to solve problems, you will capture data from specific strategic points that encompass the problem area and review that data. As an example, you can see specific detail in the Wireshark summary as shown in Figure 1.4. Here you can see specifics on the time of capture. Why this is relevant is because you have to capture data at the time of problem to find a problem. Data captured outside of this time can be used to baseline your network or its performance during normal use, but you will have to "hope" that the problem occurred at that time and/or filter the data to find it if it did in fact take place.

In Figure 1.4, we can see how many packets were captured (unfiltered), how long other specifics commonly used to identify the capture.

Figure 1.4 Wireshark capture summary.

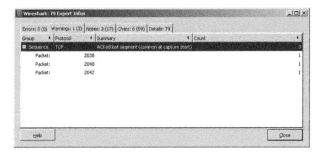

Figure 1.5 Using the Wireshark expert analysis tabs.

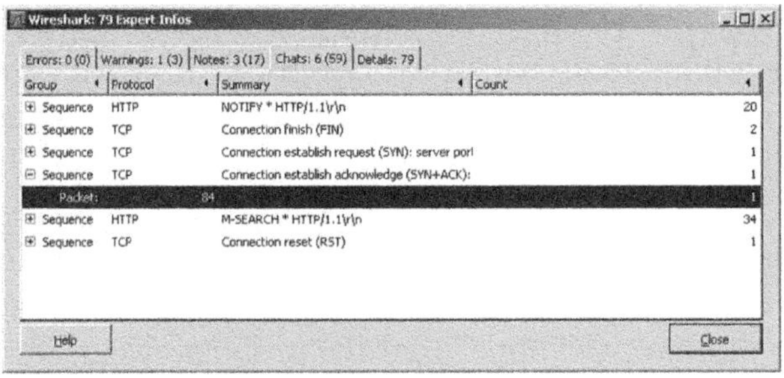

Figure 1.6 Viewing problems with Wireshark expert.

Figure 1.5 shows another tool you can use within the Wireshark program. For example, let us say you had an issue and wanted to get Wireshark's opinion as to what it thinks the problem could be. You can ask the Expert and find out. Although this is not always accurate information due to false positives, you can start to gain clues. Data traversing your network may be flagged as problematic, but it may be the way the data functions normally so therefore it may not indicate a problem, or point out the specific problem that was reported.

Figure 1.6 shows more granular data that can be obtained from Wireshark's Expert. Here we can review more "hints," but more so we can drill down further from this tool back into Wireshark's Summary pane to go directly to the packet that was flagged in order to generate an Expert message or alert.

In Figure 1.6, we can see specific problems that may be occurring in sequencing. Another helpful tip would be to expand the sequence data that was flagged and double click the packet flagged to inspect that specific packet in the Summary, Detail, and Hex panes.

Do not always trust what Wireshark tells you. False positives can mislead you. It may steer you in the wrong direction. It is, however, a good way for you to begin using the tool in order to better understand your network, the data traversing it, and the TCP/IP stack.

1.7 THE OSI MODEL

The open systems interconnection (OSI) model is used to provide a methodical way to approach how data traverses networks, systems, and operates with application used on those computers and networks. It is a helpful tool that seems to be timeless as it is continuously referenced and used today since its inception many years ago. Founded from the Department of Defense (DoD) four-layer model back when the Internet (ARPAnet) was first conceived, it serves as a way to help not only describe how data traverses systems and networks but also an outstanding tool that can be used to help troubleshoot problems.

When the data arrives at its destination, the receiving station's physical layer picks it up and performs the reverse process (also known as decapsulation). The physical layer converts the bits back into frames to pass on to the data link layer. The data link layer removes its header and trailer and passes the data on to the network layer. Once again, this process repeats itself until the data reaches all the way to the application layer. In Figure 1.7, we see the layers of the OSI model.

The layers of the OSI model are described as follows:

Application layer: This topmost layer of the OSI model is responsible for managing communications between network applications. This layer is not the application itself, although some applications may perform application layer functions. Examples of application layer protocols include file transfer protocol (FTP), hypertext transfer protocol (HTTP), simple mail transfer protocol (SMTP), and Telnet.
Presentation layer: This layer is responsible for data presentation, encryption, and compression.
Session layer: The session layer is responsible for creating and managing sessions between end systems. The session layer protocol is often unused in many protocols. Examples of protocols at the session layer include NetBIOS and remote procedure call (RPC).

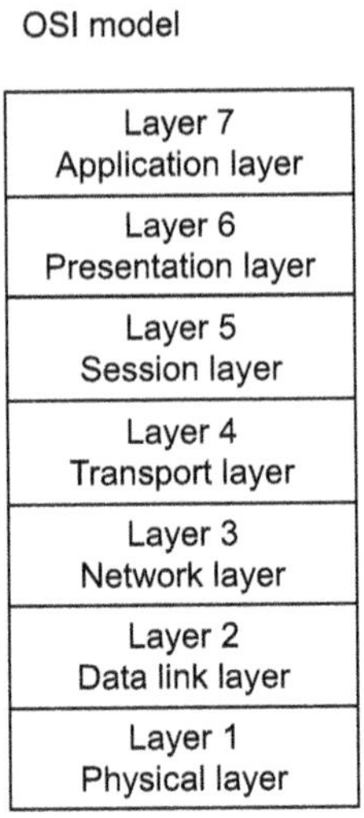

OSI model

Layer 7 Application layer
Layer 6 Presentation layer
Layer 5 Session layer
Layer 4 Transport layer
Layer 3 Network layer
Layer 2 Data link layer
Layer 1 Physical layer

Figure 1.7 The OSI model.

Transport layer: This layer is responsible for communication between programs or processes. Port or socket numbers are used to identify these unique processes. Examples of transport layer protocols include TCP, user datagram protocol (UDP), and SPX.

Network layer: This layer is responsible for addressing and delivering packets from the source node to the destination node. The network layer takes data from the transport layer and wraps it inside a packet or datagram. Logical network addresses are generally assigned to nodes at this layer. Examples of network layer protocols include IP and IPX.

Data link layer: This layer is responsible for delivering frames between NICs on the same physical segment. It is subdivided into the media access control (MAC) layer and the logical link control (LLC) layer. Communication at the data link layer is generally based on hardware addresses. The data link layer wraps data from the network layer inside a frame. Examples of data link layer protocols include Ethernet, the now almost defunct token ring, and point-to-point protocol (PPP). Devices that operate at this layer include bridges and switches.

Physical layer: This layer defines connectors, wiring, and the specifications on how voltage and bits pass over the wired (or wireless) media. Devices at this layer include repeaters, concentrators, and hubs. Devices that operate at the physical layer do not have an understanding of paths.

When using Wireshark, you must consider the methodologies used to troubleshoot with as well as how the data works on networks and systems. Knowing how to launch and run the tool is not enough! You need to specifically know where to place it, when to run it, and what it is you will capture. You will then need to analyze which tests your knowledge of networks, computers, applications, and systems.

1.8 SUMMARY

In this chapter, we have learned about protocol capture and analysis, learned the fundamentals of Wireshark as well as the fundamentals of troubleshooting with it. In the next chapter, we will learn how to install and setup Wireshark so that you can begin to use and work with it.

CHAPTER 2

Installing Wireshark

2.1 INTRODUCTION

Understanding a network, how it works and why we use tools such as Wireshark is only the beginning ... now we must build our toolkit in order to get to work. In this chapter of the book we will cover how to get Wireshark, install it, and set it up for use on a computer. We will cover how the tool changes your NIC so that it can capture data, specifically what requirements would be needed in order to not only install but use Wireshark in production as well as many other tidbits of information to make your troubleshooting time painless and productive. We will briefly go over the interface and how to launch and use the tool.

To use this field guide to its fullest potential, you must have a working Wireshark instance running on a computer system that is stable and virus-free. It is assumed that before you begin installing Wireshark for use, that your computer is network-capable and fully operational. Wireshark uses a lot of system resources, so make sure that whatever system you choose to work with is one you can preferably dedicate to this task alone. It is also recommended that any computer system you use for the purpose of packet capture and analysis be one that is portable whenever possible.

2.2 GETTING STARTED

Now that we have covered the basics and have an overview of what Wireshark can do for you and where you are going to apply this technology, next we need to get the product installed and running on a computer system so we can use it. In this chapter, you will learn how to acquire, prep, and install Wireshark.

First, you will need to consider where you will install Wireshark. There are many options for placement. For example, if you were troubleshooting a client to server connection problem on your network, you can simply install Wireshark on the offending client and problematic server. Since you don't know where the problem is and/or if it's the client or server itself, you need to do some investigation work. Once you figure out your placement points, download or copy the Wireshark executable program to each system and run the installation until completed. This is typical of how to use Wireshark and common practice for most network engineers. Figure 2.1 shows a very simplistic network segment with two client computer systems and two server systems connected together with a network switch.

Although this is a simplistic diagram and the network seems small, it doesn't change much when planning the installation of Wireshark on a large-scale enterprise network. Even if you had wide area network connections, firewalls and layers of network components between the client

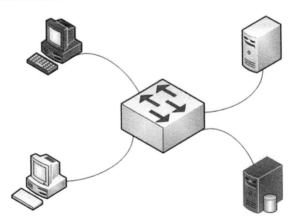

Figure 2.1 Planning Wireshark placement.

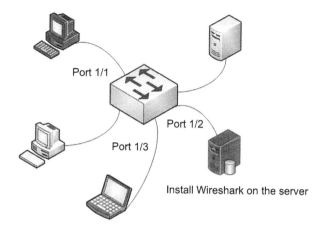

Port 1/1

Port 1/2

Port 1/3

Install Wireshark on the server

Wireshark installed on mobile system

Figure 2.2 Planning Wireshark placement.

and the server, you would still want to place Wireshark on the same systems you are having problems with. What changes is how you will read the captures taking into consideration all of the complexity found between the problem hosts.

Another common option and the one we will model our installation after here in this chapter is the preparation of a mobile computer (such as a laptop) that you can take with you and configure on the network for use. This is a more complicated way to use Wireshark, however, the least intrusive to your systems. Figure 2.2 shows a very simplistic network segment with two client computer systems and two server systems connected together with a network switch. In this scenario, we will not install Wireshark on the client system having a problem found on port 1/1 of the network switch and instead use Wireshark connected on port 1/3. The server on port 1/2 for purposes of this discussion will have Wireshark installed on it.

In this scenario, you would have to apply a secondary configuration on the network switch to send traffic from port 1/1 to port 1/3 for Wireshark to capture. This is called port spanning and/or port mirroring. We will cover this in depth in Chapter 3.

Not all network switches support port spanning or mirroring. There are other ways to perform analysis and we will cover these steps in Chapter 3.

The point to be made here is this ... you will need to know how to install and configure Wireshark for use in and around your network (or a client's network) without fail and configure it as well on adjacent systems for you to get the most out of it. Let's take a look at what requirements are needed to get Wireshark up and running anywhere on the network.

If you do not set up the software correctly, you might not get accurate data. If you do not span a port, you may not capture the traffic you intend to see, if you install Wireshark on a system that cannot use Wireshark you might not see accurate data; if this data is not picked up with a promiscuously set NIC, you will not receive accurate data to help solve a problem. If you do not span a port you may not capture network traffic destined for a specific host. Although we will continue to learn the specifics of this throughout the book it is important to reinforce these facts before installing and using Wireshark.

2.3 REQUIREMENTS

As we just learned, you may be tasked with installing Wireshark more than just once. Therefore, it's imperative to learn what you need to get it running quickly and how much pressure it puts on your system. Let's cover a few important pieces of information that are vital to your successful use of Wireshark.

- If your system does not have proper hardware resources it will not be able to run Wireshark.
- If your system is not stable it may crash while running Wireshark.
- If your system is not compatible (software and hardware) you will not be able to install or have problems after installation.
- You need administrative rights to the system in which you will install Wireshark on.

Make sure you have a large disk drive and plenty of memory to run Wireshark and capture data. A large disk drive is needed for running and storing large captures that take up a lot of disk space.

●●●

When running a capture using Wireshark, try to shut down and/or not use any other nonessential applications to conserve hardware resources such as memory, disk space, and CPU.

2.4 INSTALLATION PREPARATION

When using Wireshark, you need to know which operating systems it can function on. If the operating system is not compatible, Wireshark might not function properly. Luckily since Wireshark is an open-source-based application, finding a compatible system is not difficult. Check the Wireshark web site to find compatibility for your operating system platform. Go to 3rd Party Packages on the download page for more information.

http://www.wireshark.org/download.html

> If you do not set up the software correctly, you might not get accurate data. If you use the wrong drivers, you might not see collisions; if these collisions are not picked up with a promiscuously set NIC, you will not receive accurate reporting data. Make sure you are using the appropriate hardware verified by the Wireshark web site.
>
> http://www.wireshark.org/docs/wsug_html_chunked/ChIntroPlatforms.html
> http://wiki.wireshark.org/CaptureSetup/NetworkMedia

In the previous section, the download link was provided for Wireshark. Once you have selected the appropriate download for your system and your system has been verified for proper resources, download Wireshark and let's get started.

2.5 INSTALLING WIRESHARK

In this example, Wireshark will be installed on a 32-bit version of Windows. Although you can install it on other systems, we will focus on the most common, the Windows operating system. Once you have downloaded the executable for the Wireshark installation procedure, simply double-click on it to execute it.

> Some versions of operating systems may have incompatibility issues. A workaround that can be used in the case of Windows 8 is to install WinPcap prior to installing Wireshark because of possible incompatibility issue.

Figure 2.3 shows that once executed, you will be provided with a security warning from Windows about the installation. Here we will

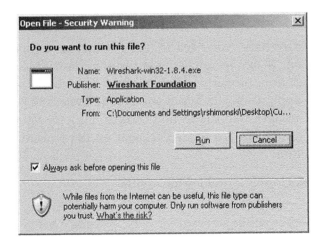

Figure 2.3 Starting the Wireshark installation.

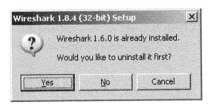

Figure 2.4 Updating Wireshark.

see that the publisher is the Wireshark Foundation and that the file is digitally signed and safe. You can always scan your files with an anti-virus program first.

In this example, we will be installing the most current version of Wireshark as of the writing of this book which is 1.8.4. This is the most current (and stable) version of the program.

You can also download and test newer versions; however, it is safer to use a stable version so that you can ensure that you are working with the more reliable version when capturing and analyzing data.

You may run into an issue when installing if you already have Wireshark installed. We will discuss this briefly. In Figure 2.4, you can see that because Wireshark is already installed on the host system, Wireshark is asking for permission to uninstall the older version before

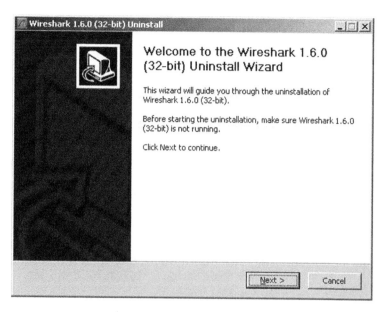

Figure 2.5 Wireshark uninstall wizard.

proceeding. By accepting and clicking on Yes, Wireshark will uninstall the older version before installing the current version.

After you agree, Wireshark will start the uninstall wizard which will walk you through removing the older version as seen in Figure 2.5. Although some programs "upgrade" the current system, Wireshark does a clean removal process and reinstallation of the new package.

Once you click Next, you will be shown the directory in which Wireshark will be removed from on your system. Normally this is found in the program file folder on your root drive. Next, you will be given options on the features you would like to uninstall. Figure 2.6 shows the options in which you can select from.

Here you can choose to keep specific components, such as WinPcap, personal settings or plug-ins. By choosing default options, you will keep personal settings and WinPcap as an example.

Take note of the drop-down menu where you can select the type of uninstall. This sets up specific options that are preset into the uninstall routine. For example, in Figure 2.7, you can select Default, All, or Custom. Quite simply, select the type of uninstall routine you want

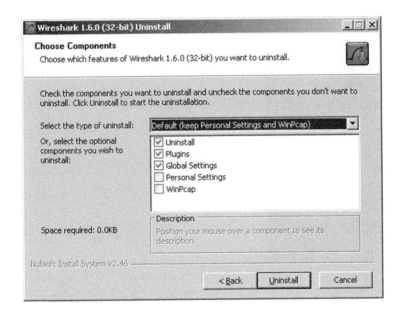

Figure 2.6 Choosing uninstall options.

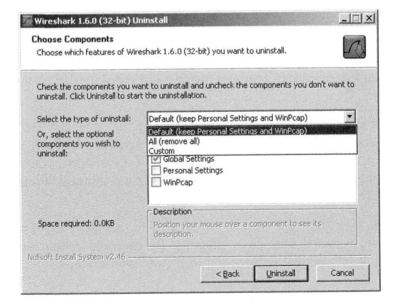

Figure 2.7 Selecting the type of uninstall.

and you can always customize the options regardless. This just makes it easier for you to select when you uninstall Wireshark.

Once you click on Uninstall, you will be shown a dialog box where you see the files and directories being removed from your system. Once it completes, select Next and you will be shown the dialog box that closes the Wizard and completes the Uninstall. Click Finish to close the wizard.

Once you have finished the uninstall, you will then invoke the Wizard to install Wireshark on your system. Figure 2.8 shows the Wireshark Setup Wizard. The current version of Wireshark (1.8.4) will be installed on the target host once you click Next.

Once you click Next, you will be shown a license agreement in which you need to select I Agree if you do to continue the installation process. Once you agree, you will then be brought the choosing components portion of the installation process. Here as seen in Figure 2.9, you can select specifically what components you would like to install.

In Figure 2.9, you are presented with the following components: Wireshark, TShark, plug-ins and extensions, tools and a user's guide.

Figure 2.8 Installing Wireshark.

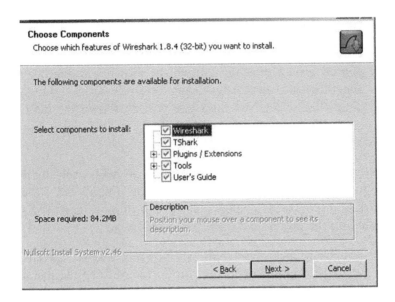

Figure 2.9 Choosing components.

You can also see that you can expand the options in the plug-ins and extensions as well as the tools components.

TShark is a terminal emulation program that you work with via the command line, much like tcpdump. To learn more about how to use TShark and the commands and switches you can use with it, please visit the Wireshark documentation for more info.

http://www.wireshark.org/docs/man-pages/tshark.html

The plug-ins component has multiple options within it. You can install Simple Network Management Protocol (SNMP) Management information bases (MIBs) as well, which are used with management software solutions that capture and alert on specific criteria. This can be helpful if you want to use Wireshark via SNMP to accomplish management and alerting tasks. Plug-in options can be seen in Figure 2.10. Select which plug-ins you would like to use and deselect those you do not want to use when preparing to install.

You can also select options within the Tools component as seen in Figure 2.11.

You can use tools, such as Editcap, Text2Pcap, and others for more. For example, Editcap is another command line tool that works

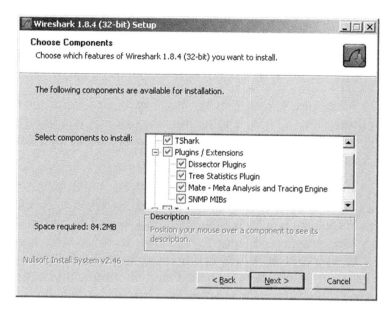

Figure 2.10 Viewing plug-in options.

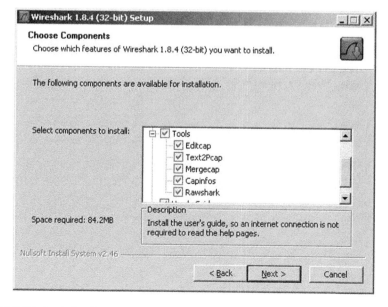

Figure 2.11 Selecting tools options.

much like a Unix input—output function where you can pipe data to files. Some technicians really enjoy the use of command line tools for many reasons; however, one of the most common of those reasons is that they can be used in scripting files that help to automate processes.

Please make sure you check your space required field in the dialog box to ensure that you have allotted for this space. If you select everything that Wireshark has to offer, you will only need approximately 85 MB for the installation to take place.

Once you have decided what components you would like to install, click Next to continue. Once you do, you will be asked to check what additional tasks you would like the Wireshark wizard to perform when installing the program. Figure 2.11 shows these specific tasks. In Figure 2.12 you can tell Wireshark upon completing installation that you want Start Menu Item's created and if specific file extensions should always be tied to Wireshark when accessed by default.

Once you click on Next, you will have to choose the directory in which to install Wireshark. By default (much like uninstall), the program file folder in the root drive will be selected. You can also see in this dialog box how much space is required and how much space you

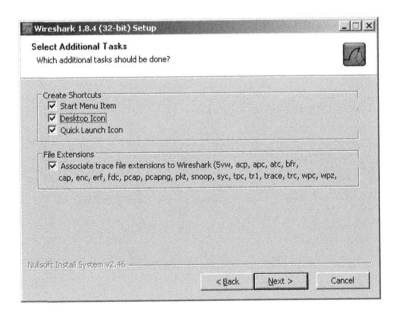

Figure 2.12 Wireshark installation tasks.

have available on the drive you wish to install it on to. Click Next to continue.

●●●

To install WinPcap on Windows 8 systems, download the executable file from http://www.winpcap.org/install/bin/WinPcap_4_1_2.exe first. Before running the file, modify the Compatibility Mode to Windows 7 within Properties. Otherwise the installation for both WinPcap and Wireshark will fail.

In Figure 2.13, we can verify if we want to install WinPcap if and only if it's a different version. For example, since we did an uninstall and WinPcap remained on the computer we are installing Wireshark on to, we have an option. For example, if this was an older version, we may be given an option to upgrade to the new version which at the time of this writing is version 4.1.2. Click on Install to install the latest version of WinPcap or upgrade it.

Next, you will be shown the extraction and installation of Wireshark and WinPcap on your Windows system. Once the installation is completed, you will be shown the final dialog box as seen in Figure 2.14. Here you can click on Finish to complete the install. If

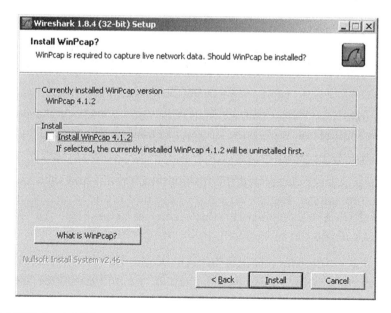

Figure 2.13 WinPcap installation.

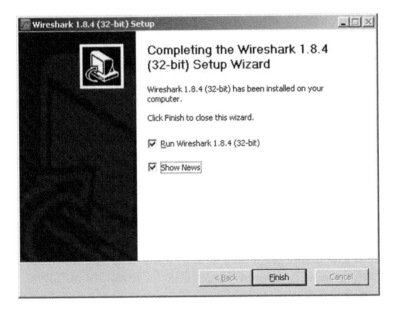

Figure 2.14 Completing the Wireshark installation.

Figure 2.15 Wireshark desktop icon.

you select the Run Wireshark or Show News check boxes, you can immediately start Wireshark as well as be shown a list of the updates and new features of Wireshark. If you are new to Wireshark, this page will be helpful to read.

Once you have completed the installation, reboot and then you can run the application. Figure 2.15 shows the desktop icon that is created postinstallation. Double-click this icon to complete the launch Wireshark if you did not select it to be run postinstallation.

You have officially installed Wireshark and have it ready to use on your computer. Now, in our next chapter, we will cover the specifics of configuring your system to prepare it for captures, filtering, and analysis of network traffic.

2.6 SUMMARY

In this chapter, we have learned about how to acquire, prepare for an installation, and conduct an installation of Wireshark. In the next chapter, we will learn how to prepare your system with Wireshark installed to capture data and conduct the appropriate analysis needed to solve problems.

CHAPTER 3

Configuring a System

3.1 INTRODUCTION

Now that we know what Wireshark does and how to get and install it, we now need to prepare it for use. Using Wireshark is not impossible, but there needs to be an understanding of what you will use it for in order to get the most out of it. For example, simply installing it on a computer and running it, capturing data, and analyzing it may help you learn more about your network the computer is connected to. You may find some protocols being used that you did not realize were in use, or verify the correct usage of the ones that you did know about. However, how would you solve a problem such as "slow response time to a server" as an example?

In this chapter, we will learn how to configure a system to use Wireshark correctly. This chapter will also learn how to correctly position it for use and provide you with sample scenarios in which Wireshark may be handy. This chapter will also cover the specifics of how to get all of the components of the network either working for you and Wireshark, or show you how to rule them out of the possible problem you may be encountering.

3.2 GETTING STARTED

Once your computer is ready to go, you will need to learn where to place Wireshark on a network. As mentioned in the last chapter, this is no simple task. In this chapter, we will cover not only configuration of network devices but also teach you how to consider the specific placement of the tool in order to use it correctly. We will learn how preparing to capture data may require making adjustments on network devices, network cabling or configuration specifics necessary to capture data. We will learn how about configuring a network device to send data to Wireshark, the correct placement and staging of the capture device(s) as well as the strategy you must plan with two end-to-end systems when more than one Wireshark capture is needed. Figure 3.1 shows a very simplistic network segment with two client computer systems connected via a network switch.

Although this is a simplistic diagram and the network seems small, this is the same methodology that we will use when working on an enterprise network. For example, if you had to use a laptop with Wireshark to analyze a connectivity problem on a server, instead of the server being connected via the same network switch as seen in Figure 3.1, imagine that server is connected across the world, across 10 router connections and 20 switches in a remote data center. It does not change the fact you still need to configure the switch the same way to send traffic to Wireshark in order for you to analyze it for any issues.

In this scenario, you would have to apply a secondary configuration on the network switch to send traffic from port 1/1 to port 1/3 for Wireshark to capture. This is called port spanning and/or port mirroring.

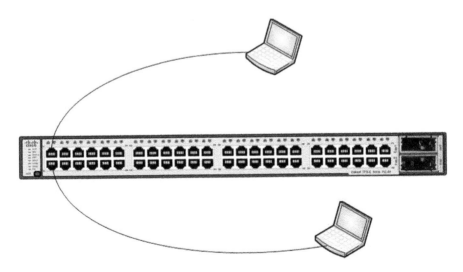

Figure 3.1 Planning Wireshark placement.

You can capture an entire conversation without impacting the systems as they work on the network by conducting this type of analysis.

Before we get into the details on how to configure mirroring, let's make sure we understand why we would do this. Let's say we wanted to troubleshoot a conversation between Computer A and Computer B as seen in Figure 3.2. For example, Computer A had a slow login to Computer B and there were no clue in obtained logs or any other method of analysis to prove why. This is where Wireshark makes its money. Connecting Wireshark to a network switch and spanning the traffic over to the computer with Wireshark installed will allow for the capture and analysis of the entire conversation in order for you to analyze it. Yes, you could install Wireshark directly on the system itself; however, there may be reasons why you may not want to or be able to. Incompatibility may be one reason. Policy may be another (your company does not allow it). You may not have access to install it on the system; therefore, mirroring and spanning may be your only alternative. Regardless, this chapter covers the final items you would need to get Wireshark up and running to use it for data capture and analysis.

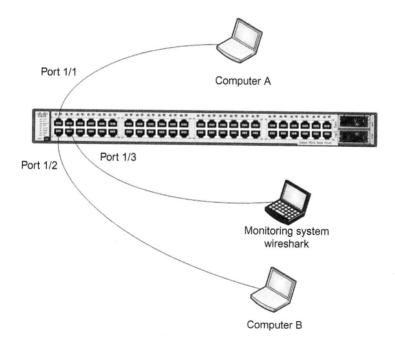

Figure 3.2 Planning Wireshark placement.

Although this chapter covers Cisco Systems switches in detail, you can in fact install mirroring and/or spanning on other systems such as a Nortel switch and many others. Cisco is the most commonly used switch today, therefore, we will cover Cisco in detail; however, if you need to configure Wireshark on a Juniper, Nortel or HP switch, please look up the configurations online as they will be similar to what is discussed here in theory.

3.3 CONFIGURING A CISCO PORT MONITOR

In this chapter, we will configure a Cisco switch to mirror traffic from one port to another for capture and data analysis. As we mentioned before, although other switches can be used in the same fashion, the same holds true for the packet capture and analysis tool itself. For example, when configure Netflow, you can use similar functions. When sending traffic, you can send it to a Fluke Packet capture device, or a Netscout repository. There are many ways you can use what is learned in this chapter as a network engineer so take note.

To configure port monitoring (also called Switched Port Analyzer or SPAN) on a Cisco Catalyst switch, first you need to know what model of switch you are using. For example, using a 2940, 2950, 2955, 2970, 3550, or 3750 series switch is different than using a switch from the Nexus line. Rest assured that there is plenty of documentation available to aid you in the configuration of any device in Cisco's product line; however, it's important to note that the commands are not completely universal.

So what does SPAN do? SPAN when configured correctly (as seen in Figure 3.2) will send a copy of the data traversing a port to another port for copy. If you have a computer system with a NIC set in promiscuous mode and a protocol analyzer configured, you can capture the data and filter and analyze it.

●●●───

Remote Monitoring (RMON) probes and other devices such as IPS units to provide secure also function this way. As we will learn, there are many ways to configure a SPAN port, not only for Wireshark but many other tools and systems that need to capture and use a copy of data traversing links for the purposes of analysis. This chapter is extremely valuable to not only learning how to use Wireshark, but to become a network engineer or security engineer in general.

SPAN mirrors can receive or transmit traffic on one or more source ports to a destination port for analysis. You can SPAN multiple ports to one destination. It does this without impacting the network or interfering with the transmission of data. There are special cases, however, when running a span of a trunk port (or port channel) on overutilized systems you may encounter resource depletion such as high CPU as an example.

Other functions of SPAN include Remote SPAN (RSPAN) which is used to extend SPAN by enabling RMON on multiple switches over an enterprise network. This can also be configured over an RSPAN Virtual Local Area Network (VLAN) used only for these types of sessions and copied via specified reflector ports. Although this is somewhat complex, it really isn't in theory, however can get a slightly complicated in application. Once configured however, also note that a network is a living entity whereas if you need to "troubleshoot" a problem somewhere on your network, you may need to move a probe, move a monitor or move a packet capture device to the problem which means that you will need to conduct configurations at that time. That being said, let's walk through the most common you will do:

1. First find where your connections map to on the network. For example, a computer or server network connection may disappear into the distance, an Intermediate Distribution Facility (IDF) or a patch panel. What you need to know is what switch port the device connects into in order to SPAN it.
2. You can always look in the switches ARP cache for the MAC address and what port it's associated to. This is extremely helpful in cases where you cannot map the connection. You may need the IP address of the source (and or destination) computer in order to map the device to a port in this fashion.
3. Once you find this information, you need to find a free port on the network to connect your analyzer (Wireshark) to in order to configure it for promiscuous capture.

Next, you will want to log into the device in which you want to configure a SPAN session. Once logged in, you will need to make administrative changes to the switch.

Before making any changes to a production network, make sure that you are authorized to do so. If you are reading a book about capturing data and analyzing it at the packet level, it's assumed you know a thing or two about working on a production network; however, this is not always the case. If you do not have experience working on a production network professionally, please do not make any of these configuration changes without first running them in a controlled lab environment first.

You first configuration is to turn off any current session monitoring if session monitoring is already in place. If you want to turn off monitoring on a particular session, simply list it by its session number.

LabSwitch1(config)# no monitor session all
LabSwitch1(config)# no monitor session 1

Next, you will want to configure session monitoring to and from the specific ports you mapped out earlier. In Figure 3.3, we see a current example of what we will be configuring on this lab switch. We will install Wireshark on Computer A (Chapter 2) and we will SPAN a port from port 2 to port 3 for a production server where we cannot install Wireshark.

This example shows how to set up a SPAN session (session 1) for monitoring source port traffic to a destination port. First, any existing SPAN configuration for session 1 is cleared and then bidirectional traffic is mirrored from source port 1/2 to destination port 1/3:

LabSwitch1(config)#   monitor   session   1   source   interface
fastEthernet1/2
LabSwitch1 (config)#   monitor   session   1   destination   interface
fastEthernet1/3
LabSwitch1 (config)# end

Now you will be able to capture data from source to destination for analysis. When you run a capture, make sure that you capture both ends of the communication real time at the same time. For example, if you wanted to find out why it takes a long time for the client (Computer A) to login to a server, you can run Wireshark on

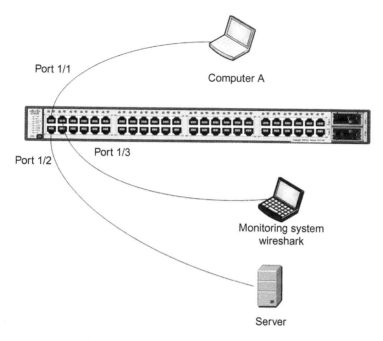

Port 1/1

Computer A

Port 1/2

Port 1/3

Monitoring system
wireshark

Server

Figure 3.3 Planning Wireshark placement.

Computer A and the monitoring device while attempting to login and then analyzing both sets of data to find root cause.

●●●

Do not forget the basics. Although Wireshark is extremely handy in finding problems, it is best used when leveraged with other tools. For example, you may want to parse the event logs on the Windows server as well as the client computer while examining the Wireshark data. You may see that a slow login problem can be identified in the event logs; however, the specific reasons (congested switch) may only show up in the Wireshark detail. Remember, even though you are troubleshooting and using Wireshark as a tool, it's not the only tool in your toolbelt. The best technicians, analysts, and engineers use server logs, infrastructure device logs, packet analysis, and many other tools to solve the most complex problems.

Once you have set Wireshark up correctly, you need to consider placement. We touched on this earlier in the book. Placement is something that takes a little time, patience, and experience to get right. For example, if someone said that they had a problem accessing data. Consider all of the areas in which you may have to consider:

- Client: The client is the most common place to start … that's where most problems are reported from. The end user could not do something like surf the Internet, use a specific application or having a hard time logging into a server. This is where you get most of your clues.
- Application: Could the application be having issues? When moving between services in the application, is the application passing multiple tiers? Is there an application layer? Would installing Wireshark on the application tier make more sense than installing it on the web services portion? What if the application is delivered using a solution such as Citrix? Do we install Wireshark on the Citrix server? Why would we?
- Database: Is the Database server the cause of the issue? What gives us this impression? Was the user doing something that caused a lock? Why would we install Wireshark on the Database server?
- Web services: Was the front end the cause of the problem?
- Cluster: Are the systems clustered? What is the active node in the cluster?
- Server: Is the server the cause of the issue? Running low on resources?
- Virtualization: Is the server a virtualized system? Is the Virtual server causing issues? Where do you install Wireshark?
- Network: Is the path congested? Is it a LAN connection problem, WAN link, or the Internet that is slow? Is the connection via a virtual private network (VPN)? Where do we install Wireshark?
- Load balancer: Are the applications or services load balanced and running through a load balancer? Where would we install Wireshark?
- Proxy services: Is the client directed to a proxy service? Is this the problem? Do we install Wireshark on the proxy?
- Firewall: Is the traffic running through a firewall or some other inspection device such as Intrusion Prevention System (IPS)/ Intrusion Detection System (IDS)?
- Name resolution: Is name resolution a cause of the issue? How would we know? Where do we install Wireshark?
- Would we use Wireshark to find out why RADIUS is problematic?

Mind you, these are just "some" of the areas in which to consider. This is why as mentioned earlier Wireshark is but a tool to be used as an extension of an experienced technicians brain. This is why using other tools such as system logs is so important. By finding clues in these logs you can narrow down where you want and may need to install and capture data with Wireshark. As you can see, it's not as easy as it may seem. It's not about how to install and use this tool, but specifically why and where.

We are almost done with Chapter 3. Chapters 1–3 simply covered what Wireshark does, how to get and install it and how to use it in the most basic format. The most important thing to consider before moving to Chapter 4 is that if you do not grasp what is covered in the first three chapters, then using it in chapters 4–10 will be useless. Unless you know where to place it and know what you are doing to capture data, analyzing the captured data is useless. For example, I have personally received one Wireshark data capture from a workstation asking me to find a problem. Not knowing what the problem is why it happened, when it happened and what the problem was specifically, it will prove fruitless. Sometimes you can glean clues, however, to truly use this tool correctly, you need to plan to use it correctly.

3.4 OTHER TOOLS AND METHODOLOGIES

When troubleshooting with Wireshark, it's recommended that you take the time to use other tools and methodologies while you are analyzing the problem. For example, in the same switches and routers you are piping the information from, you can use commands on them to help find the problem. Although there are books and many online articles that cover these in more detail, for the purposes of this field guide we will help you develop the methodology instead of specifically stating what those commands may be. For example, if you find you have a user complaining of an application that seems to freeze up or appear sluggish, you can do the following tests in phases of complexity:

Phase 1 Testing (quick checks, somewhat nonintrusive)
1. First try to understand what the problem is by framing it. Ask as many questions as needed. Put on the private investigator hat and attempt to capture the end user's experience.
2. Next verify that no changes were made that could impact.
3. Verify path and check all devices in the path. Check logs.

4. You can then look over the basics. Ping, traceroute, advanced ping commands where you can specific packet sizes will help you to provide a load (to test fragmentation) as an example.

5. Checking performance. Bandwidth, CPU, it can get as deep as checking performance on a storage area network (SAN).

6. You could install and use Wireshark at this point, however.

7. You can run checks on the network devices and infrastructure—look at the logs, run basic checks with specific commands that highlight—run nonintrusive debugs

Phase 2 Testing (deeper level of inspection and more time consuming and may be intrusive)

1. Wireshark set up on both ends from source to destination, checking the timing of the packets from source to destination. This is more difficult to perform because you need access to both systems (as an example) and will have to run the tests in tandem. You will have to analyze both captures using timestamps in order to verify when data was sent and when it was received and any errors or anomalies that took place during that period of time. When analyzing timestamps a recommended procedure would be to ensure that all devices you run Wireshark on have the correct time which can be done through configuring Network Time Protocol (NTP), or the Windows Time Service (W32Time).

2. Real-time analysis of traffic and deep inspection by looking into packet headers will uncover a more granular level of detail, however, will take more time to review and analyze.

3. Run intrusive tests such as performance test on network links that will verify the validity of the bandwidth and size however will inadvertently shut down the link for use thus causing an outage.

4. Run heavy debugs on infrastructure devices. This may cause the device to process heavily therefore spike the CPU and cause the device to perform poorly (if at all) to process production traffic.

5. Other tests to conduct would be to reboot physical servers, move cluster nodes from primary to secondary, moving virtual machine (VM instances) from one host to another and other "server-related" testing that may help isolate the issue.

6. Cabling testing where cables need to be replaced or verified may cause a disruption or an outage if not redundant.

Although I created a framework for this methodology and called it phased testing, it's nothing more than how normal network engineers

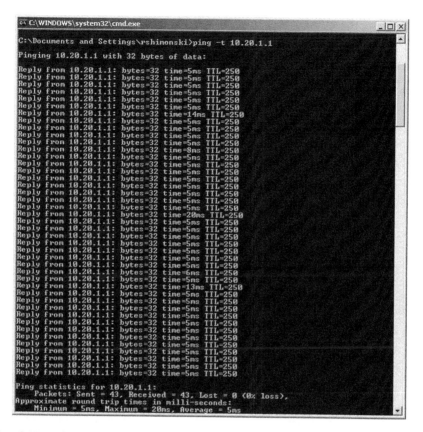

Figure 3.4 Using the ping command.

perform their jobs every day. As you can see from this example, using Wireshark is not the only tool used to solve problems, its only one of the many different tools (or processes) used to solve simple to complex problems every day. Figures 3.4 and 3.5 show examples of other testing methods you can deploy with Wireshark to solve a problem.

In Figure 3.4, we see an example of using the ping command to test connectivity as well as the stability of a network connection. This can be used to help assess if bandwidth or latency can be an issue with for example, a slow application response time. If the application is slow to respond and the network is suspect, by running a quick ping from the source to the destination can quickly help rule out what the network looks like and is performing in seconds.

In Figure 3.5 we see an example of another helpful tool called the SolarWinds Engineer's Toolset. This tool much like the rest of the

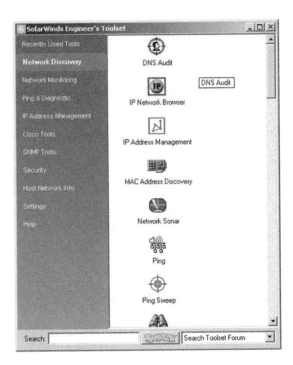

Figure 3.5 SolarWinds engineer's toolset.

SolarWinds product line make network management and troubleshooting easier; for example, you can run a ping sweep of a subnet to verify connectivity of a device or devices quickly and easily through the GUI.

In sum, remember that Wireshark is but one tool—and using it alone can be helpful but when used in conjunction with other tools can help solve problems quicker. It should also be considered that when troubleshooting, you have to learn "where" to place your packet analyzers so that you can collect the correct data. You also have to time the problem correctly and sometimes collect baseline data to ensure you can understand how the network performs normally before you can suspect a problem.

3.5 SUMMARY

In this chapter, we have learned about protocol capture and analysis learned the fundamentals of Wireshark as well as the fundamentals of troubleshooting with it. In the next chapter, we will learn how to use Wireshark once data is captured and how to analyze specific data.

Capturing Packets

4.1 INTRODUCTION

In the last three chapters, we covered the fundamental basics of Wireshark and how to get it up and running on a computer system and/or network. We covered how to set it up so that you can capture packets and begin to analyze them. In this chapter, we will start to use Wireshark to capture those packets to troubleshoot problems. Capturing packets is a fairly easy concept to digest once your system is up and running correctly and you understand what Wireshark does.

In this chapter, we will learn how to capture data and how to view it within Wireshark so that you can start solving problems. Packet analysis starts with the inspection of packets, however, if you do not capture the data correctly you will have a tough time understanding what you are looking at or finding what you need. There are also many ways you can approach the capturing of this data.

Wireshark can be used to capture packets on a computer network via the NIC in promiscuous mode. This means that all data traversing the network and touching this interface can and will be recorded. As we mentioned with spanned ports in the previous chapter, you can also set up Wireshark to collect data from a particular port. That being said, make sure you have permission to do so. You could be doing this against policy if you are not authorized to do so.

4.2 GETTING STARTED

In this chapter, we will learn the art of capturing packets in order to decode them, analyze them, and inspect what is traversing your network. Once you have started to capture packets, the rest of the chapters leading up to the last chapter (saving captures and saving files), you will be learning about the interface and how to manipulate it to troubleshoot problems. This chapter covers more of what you learnt in Chapter 1 about the three panes and all details within them, running captures as well as how to start and stop Wireshark. We will also review a sample problem.

To start capturing packets, simply open Wireshark on your computer as shown in Figure 4.1. In the window, you will find the Capture section in the top left pane. You can view the Interface List, Start a capture based on a particular interface and set Capture Options.

As we have learned, there are many things you can do with Wireshark and in this chapter, we will expand on all the ways you can capture packets. It should be noted that you can also use the Files pane in the middle of the window as shown in Figure 4.1 to open previously saved captures or click on the Sample Captures link to go online and view the saved repository of samples.

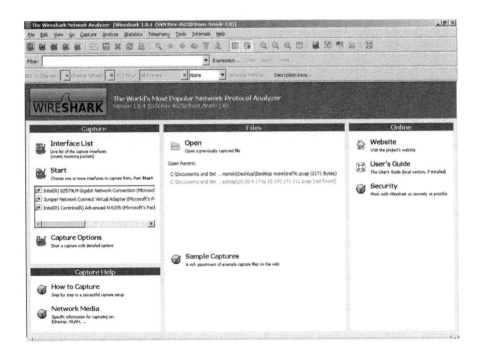

Figure 4.1 Opening Wireshark to capture packets.

If you are very interested in learning about Wireshark, protocol analysis, or networking in general, it is highly advisable that you visit this online repository of samples. Here you can see a large set of captures that show specific types of protocol behavior: http://wiki.wireshark.org/CaptureFilters.

As an example, if you want to learn more about how dynamic host configuration protocol (DHCP) operates (and looks like in a capture), simply download the capture files and open them within the Files pane link. Since this is only a field guide, we cannot get too deep into every little detail, so this is a great way to augment your studies and learn more about the Wireshark tool.

Once you have opened Wireshark and want to start to run a capture, the first step would be to select an interface (NIC) in which you want to capture on. As shown in Figure 4.1, there are commonly more than one interface on any given machine you may work with. For example, on the system where captures will be taken here, there is a physical NIC, a virtual NIC (VPN connection) and a Wireless NIC. You can click on the Interface List link to produce the Wireshark Capture Interfaces dialog box as shown in Figure 4.2.

Once you open this dialog box, you will be presented with a full set of functional network connections configured on your computer. You can put a checkbox into the interface you would like to select. For this example, we will select the physical NIC which is an Intel Gigabit NIC. You can further drill down into the interface specifics by clicking on the Details button found within the Wireshark Capture Interfaces dialog box to produce the Wireshark Interface Details dialog box as shown in Figure 4.3.

This dialog box can be very helpful if you need to check specific information about your NIC card. For example, if you want to verify information about your NIC that may be relevant to the capture data,

Figure 4.2 The Wireshark Capture Interfaces dialog box.

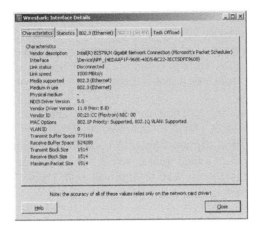

Figure 4.3 The Wireshark Interface Details dialog box.

such as the maximum transmission unit (MTU) size, the MAC address, or the vendor specifics, this information can be found here as well as a series of other relevant data, such as real-time statistics and so on. You can close out this dialog box once you have reviewed it.

Figure 4.4 shows the Wireshark Capture Options dialog box. This can be found by clicking on the Wireshark Capture Options link found in the Capture pane of the Wireshark landing page as shown in Figure 4.1.

This dialog box is also very helpful when it comes to starting (and stopping) a packet capture. For example, you can not only select the interfaces and manage them (such as configuring local and remote interfaces as well as pipes) but also set Wireshark to capture on all interfaces, specific files in which to capture, set a limit on how much data you want to capture in each file and so on.

As was mentioned earlier in the book, capture files can grow quite large. They can not only grow to the size of your hard disk (as a concern) but also grow too large to adequately inspect without specific filtering. The "Use Multiple Files" option is a great way to control the size of the captures in a way that you can limit and control these factors.

While in the Wireshark Capture Options dialog box (as shown in Figure 4.4), you can also double click on one of the interfaces

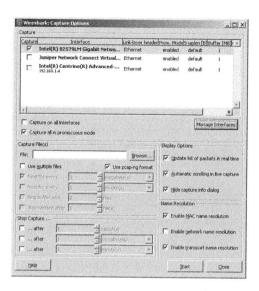

Figure 4.4 Wireshark capture options.

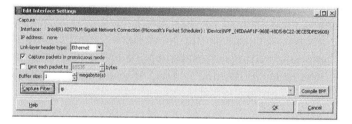

Figure 4.5 The Edit Interface Settings dialog box.

themselves in the top pane to make additional settings adjustments. In Figure 4.5, you will find the Edit Interface Settings dialog box. Here you can change the Link-layer header type, set buffering options, or configure a capture filter on that particular interface.

We will learn more about capture filters in a future chapter, however, as a general explanation here, a capture filter is nothing more than a configured filter that will allow you to refine your capture details. As an example seen in Figure 4.5, we will only allow for the IP to be captured on this particular interface. If you click on the Capture Filter button, you will open the Wireshark Capture Filter (Profile Default) dialog box as shown in Figure 4.6. In this specific example, I am setting a specific Filter Name and Filter String in the fields found

Figure 4.6 The Wireshark Capture Filter Profile dialog box.

within Properties. This means I am going to set a specific capture of a system (IP address 10.1.1.2) using Telnet.

Click OK or Cancel to save your filter. Click OK to save your choices, and/or click Cancel to close the Edit Interface Settings dialog box which brings you back to the Wireshark Capture Options dialog box. You can make settings changes here or leave everything as default and click Close to leave the dialog box, or you can click the Start button to begin your capture.

Once you start your capture, Wireshark will open the Interface you specified using the Wireshark capture window as shown in Figure 4.7. As we reviewed in Chapter 1, there are three panes: Summary, Detail, and Hex.

Once you start the capture, you will see some specific behavior, such as packets being timestamped and captured in order as seen in the capture window. A timestamp (found in the Time column) denotes when specifically the packet was captured in succession. You will also find the source and destination addresses of each packet captured in the Source and Destination columns.

Next, you will find the specific protocol in use in the Protocol column, such as IP (and version), TCP, UDP, and DHCP. Beyond the protocol designation is the Length column, which shows you the specific packet length. Earlier we mentioned MTU, which denotes the maximum size that a packet can be sent before it fragments.

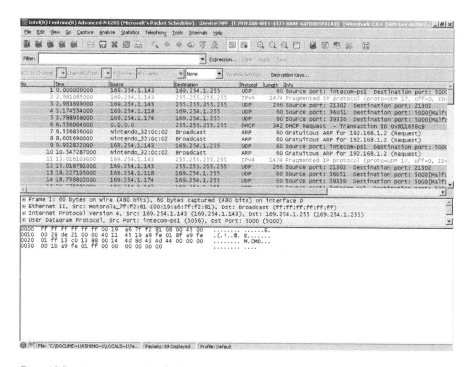

Figure 4.7 Starting a capture in Wireshark.

●●●

The size of the packets can also be problematic. If you find that most of your packets traversing your interface are small packets, which means that the interface itself has more to do to process each packet (usually for reassembly) and handle encapsulation.

Fragmented packets can become a problem. IP packets can be fragmented from their original size into smaller chunks for transmission over a network. They need to be reassembled which causes more work for the device handling this task.

It is also recommended that you learn more about the actual packets you will capture and inspect, and there is no better starting point than Internet RFCs or Request for Comment files. This one covers IP and details the issues behind fragmentation: http://tools.ietf.org/html/rfc791.

The Info column highlights particular information you may need to know about the packet that was captured. For example, in the case of the captured ARP packets, it was helpful to learn that it was a gratuitous ARP and simply a request. This covers the details of the Summary pane. The Details pane simply breaks down each packet

Figure 4.8 The Wireshark Open Capture File dialog box.

into more granular data (which we will review in upcoming chapters) and the Hex pane does the same with each section of the Details pane.

Since we started the capture via the landing page, you can stop the capture within the Wireshark capture window. To operate the capture from within this window, there is a toolbar at the top of the screen as well as a menu system. You can select the Capture menu option to start and stop captures. You can also use the capture icons to start and stop the capture on the toolbar. There are other options in this menu and the toolbar to review. Some of them are "restarting" a capture after you initially stop it. You can also start a new capture if needed.

We will cover the saving of a file in the last chapter as there are many options that revolve around it, however for purposes here, simply go to the File menu and select Save.

To open a saved capture, you will find the last capture you took in the landing page under Files. Once you click on the link, the Wireshark Open Capture File dialog box will open as shown in Figure 4.8.

In the example shown in Figure 4.9, I have downloaded a sample NTP synchronization sample to open within the Wireshark capture window for review.

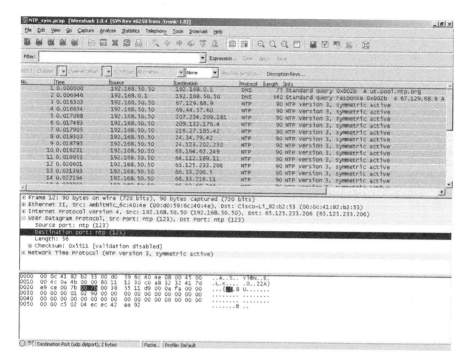

Figure 4.9 Viewing an NTP capture file.

In the example, we will review how an NTP (time synchronization) transfer between source and destination should look like and analyze why there may be a problem, or if it is working as it should.

In the example, we see no problems in this synchronization of a clock on the 192.168.50.x network using a public Internet time source. It is using port 123 as seen in the Details pane data (source and destination port). What could have gone wrong? The connection to the network could have been local with no Internet access therefore not allowing the sync to take place. A firewall (either locally or remote) could have been blocking this IP range and/or the NTP port 123.

4.3 SUMMARY

In this chapter, we covered how to get start with Wireshark—to launch it, configure it to capture and start capturing data. Now we have learned how to capture protocol data within Wireshark. Next, we will cover how to start to view, manipulate, filter, and analyze what you are capturing.

CHAPTER 5

Color Codes

In this chapter, we will learn how to customize your captures. This chapter will be a segue into the next chapter, which will cover creating filters. In Chapter 4, we have covered the basics of performing a capture and learned how to set up a quick filter on your profile's default configuration. In this chapter, we will learn how to further your captures in a visual representation for quick and easy viewing purposes.

Wireshark is a very visual tool. The tool includes prebuilt filters and coloring codes, and it lets you create new ones or edit the ones already in place. As you will see, it is extremely flexible. When working with Wireshark, you will see that when capturing packets, the amount of data can become unwieldy most times. A quick and easy way to interpret what you are viewing is to view (and understand) how Wireshark color codes packets. Once you have used the tool long enough, you will find that by simply seeing a color, you will already know specific details about the packets you are capturing without having to read the contents of each one to get a general understanding of what is taking place on your network.

5.1 GETTING STARTED

Deeper inspection within the capture is required. In this chapter, we will learn how Wireshark color codes the captures and how we can quickly look for problems. We will also learn more about protocols, ports, and other critical network-based information that help solve problems.

First, we have to understand why we color code. The easiest answer to this question is to make it easier for use as problem solvers and to more quickly visualize problems on our network. That being said, Wireshark allows us to do this by expanding what is already available by default using custom color coding schemes. There are two types of color coding profiles you can use with Wireshark. One is temporary and the other is one that can be kept by Wireshark to be used each and every time you use the system.

Do not worry about making changes to the defaults of Wireshark; you can always reset your work and remove any of the custom color coding profile data you insert by clearing any and all changes. You will learn how to do this in this chapter.

5.2 CREATING COLOR CODE LISTS

To get started, open the last capture you took or create a new capture file. Once you are done capturing data, go to the View menu in the Wireshark capture window. Select the Coloring Rules option from the menu. You will open the Wireshark Coloring Rules (Profile Default) dialog box as shown in Figure 5.1.

Here, you will find many predefined filter sets as shown in Figure 5.1. In the middle window, you will see a list of filters denoted as Name and String. The string is the "action" that Wireshark is taking when it applies this filter. It should also be noted that the list is processed from top to down and goes in that order until a match is made and processed.

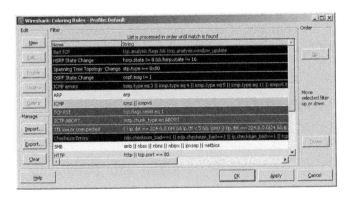

Figure 5.1 The Wireshark Coloring Rules dialog box.

On the left side of the dialog box is the Edit area. Here, you can create a new color code filter, edit a preexisting one, enable or disable one, or remove one completely. If you choose to create a new color code filter, click on the New button as shown in Figure 5.1. This will open the Wireshark Edit Color Filter dialog box as shown in Figure 5.2.

In this example, a filter that specifically highlights a particular IP address in yellow font with a blue background was created for quick and easy viewing. Before we get into how we created this filter, it should be apparent as to why and how this could be extremely helpful. In this instance, let us say you were troubleshooting a specific IP address that you wanted to view in your capture and isolate. Now, visually you can see when that IP address is found in a packet that Wireshark captures by viewing the Summary Pane in the Wireshark capture window. How was this created? Simple, here is how it was done.

> When making filters, try to use a color coding scheme that is visible to you as well; try not to duplicate anything else already in use.

Open the Display Colors by selecting either the Foreground Color or Background Color buttons as shown in Figure 5.2. In Figure 5.2, we see the Wireshark Choose Foreground Color dialog box open where you can select the written font color; here yellow color was chosen. Click on the eyedropper icon and then on the color map in the left-hand side of the dialog box and select the color, or if you know Hex coloring schemes (Figure 5.3), you can configure it in the color "name" field within the dialog box.

Follow the same method for the background color and then choose OK.

Once you have completed these steps, you need to configure the actual filter in which you will capture data. You can do this by

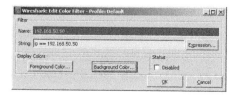

Figure 5.2 The Wireshark Edit Color Filter dialog box.

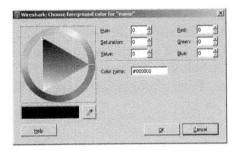

Figure 5.3 The Wireshark Choose Foreground Color dialog box.

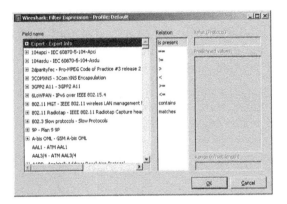

Figure 5.4 The Wireshark Filter Expression dialog box.

clicking on Expression as shown in Figure 5.2. This will open the dialog box as shown in Figure 5.4. Here, you will find the Wireshark Filter Expression dialog box.

If you know how to enter the string manually, you do not need to open the dialog box; however, if you are new to Wireshark and to applying filters, there is no better way to learn than to using this dialog box. Here, you can select the field name and then the relation which is nothing more than applying Boolean math to your selection criteria. For example, if you want to capture an address that is equal to a specific value, it would look similar to

ip = =192.168.50.50

Once you have finished, you can click on OK two times to get back to the Wireshark Coloring Rule dialog box as shown in Figure 5.5. Here, you will find the new filter applied to the rules filter list.

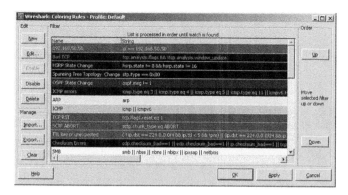

Figure 5.5 The Wireshark Coloring Rules dialog box.

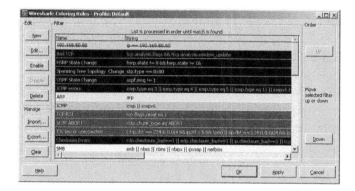

Figure 5.6 Disabling a Wireshark color code filter.

Now, you can see the new rule applied which, when you run a new capture, can be used to color code that specific data in the Wireshark capture window for easy viewing.

You can use the Order section on the right side of the dialog box to move rules up or down in the list if you want to decrease the processing that Wireshark will have to do in order to match your data against the filter list.

5.3 ADDING AND REMOVING FILTERS

You can disable a filter by selecting it with your mouse and then clicking on the Disable button in the Edit section. Once you have done so, the filter will be crossed out and disabled (but not removed) from the processing list, which is shown in Figure 5.6.

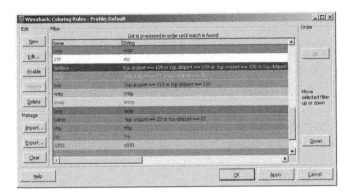

Figure 5.7 Viewing an imported color code list.

You can select Enable to enable it, or Delete to remove it from the list. One last feature we review here is the importing and exporting of color code lists that were already made and found on the Wireshark Wiki. This is incredibly handy when you want to build lists, where it would take you a lot of time in minutes. You can also export your custom lists to either submit to the Wiki and/or use in your own groups, give to peers, or use to help others as needed. To import a list, you first need to get the list you will import.

To do this, you can visit the online list repository where there are many capture filters available:

http://wiki.wireshark.org/ColoringRules

Once you download a list that you find may be helpful, simply click on the Import button and browse to the import list file. Once completed and imported, you will see it in your Wireshark Coloring Rules dialog box as shown in Figure 5.7.

In this example, we have configured Wireshark to capture data and color code it specifically as seen in the filter list. Now, if you have an e-mail problem and you are trying to view packets using SMTP or POP, they will show up colored pink with white font or black font.

Again, this is just a way for you to quickly visualize a problem and make it easier to troubleshoot. This book intends on getting you up to run and use Wireshark quickly for the purpose of solving problems. The keywords here are "quick" and "easy." There is nothing simple about this program; however, it is designed very well to make using it

Figure 5.8 Removing all personal color settings dialog box.

very digestible. Color coding is one such way where this is accomplished.

Once you have test driven your new color code filters, you can always reset Wireshark back to custom defaults easily. To do this, you can open the Wireshark Coloring Rules dialog box backup and click on the Clear button in the Manage section, which will allow you to clear all your rules as shown in Figure 5.8. Click Clear to remove all settings from the global default profile.

5.4 OTHER COLORING OPTIONS

Wireshark also allows you to apply color in another way to help you isolate problems. In this example, we will look at conversations such as source IP address and destination IP address as shown in Figure 5.9. Here, click on the View menu option and scroll down to Colorize Conversation and expand the menu to view the coloring options.

What this helps you do is "mark" conversations in a capture file for easy viewing. Now, to do this, simply click on a conversation pair found in one packet in the Summary pane. Next, click on the View menu option, Colorize Conversation, and select Color 1.

This will then mark every packet in the capture having this conversation with that specific color code you have chosen. This is very helpful when you are trying to quickly visualize that particular conversation in a large capture file.

5.5 SUMMARY

In this chapter, we have discussed how you can customize Wireshark with color coding in order to mark specific data you are capturing and/or have captured. This is essential when you try to solve problems

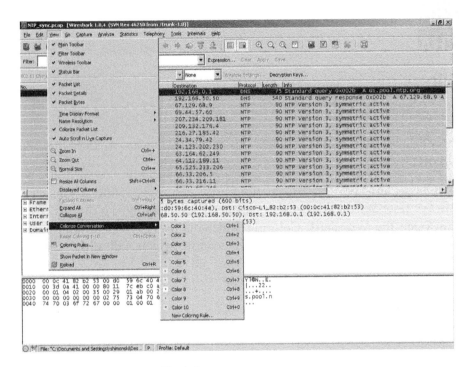

Figure 5.9 Coloring Conversation in Wireshark.

quickly in the field and need to use your visual skills to interpret problems while working in the Summary pane of the Wireshark capture
window. In Chapter 6, we will expand our discussion on filters to go
more in depth on using filtering options to capture and sort your captured data to perform protocol analysis.

Filters

In this chapter, we will learn how to filter data in Wireshark to troubleshoot problems. How to filter captures correctly is the key to finding problems especially when running Wireshark on networks where a lot of data traverses. Consider capturing data from one system communicating with another... what would you specifically search for to help solve a problem? Filtering on protocols, IP addresses, and using specific Boolean arguments are covered as well as specific example of filters that you can use right away to help get you up and running and working with Wireshark immediately.

When it comes to networks, you can separate out unnecessary data, data irrelevant to the problem or the event that we are exploring. The most important and the most difficult thing to do is not to capture data but to find out which of the thousands of packets traversing your network are related to a problem you are working on, diagnose the problem correctly, and prove out the problem to move directly to eliminating its cause. Wireshark is a very good tool to perform this troubleshooting as long as you choose the correct filter to help sort through (or initially capture) the relevant data needed. Choosing (or creating) the correct filter will make your life easier when it comes to scanning the data and analyzing it for problems and that is what we will cover specifically in this chapter.

If you incorrectly define a filter, you may in adversely omit criteria you want to search for therefore making what you are looking for even harder to find.

6.1 GETTING STARTED

In the data transmission environment, filtering becomes very important when it comes to the search and use of specific information hidden in the midst of unimportant data. One of the most difficult and significant task involved in working with Wireshark is to define the right filter. Having defined a correct filter, you will be able to save a great deal of time when it comes to detecting a problem on your network or analyzing data you have captured using a particular filter. Different types of filtering are available: You can filter traffic based on Layer 2 and Layer 3 addresses, protocol types, and/or data patterns.

●●●

To learn more about the specifics of filtering above and beyond this field guide's capacity, it is recommended that you read the filtering section on the Wireshark Wiki: http://wiki.wireshark.org/CaptureFilters

Here you will find useful information that can help you create filters as well as find a repository of already predefined capture filters that can assist you in your studies or work.

6.2 APPLYING A FILTER

Applying a filter can be done in many ways. First, we learnt in earlier chapters that when running a capture you can simply apply a filter to the profile's default configuration. This will apply once you begin your relevant captures. You can also apply a filter before running a capture and/or apply a filter after you run a capture. We already covered the profile default in Chapter 4.

In this chapter, we will learn how to apply a filter before and after running a capture. You can apply a filter prior to running a capture and after as we learnt in Chapters 4 and 5. In this chapter, we will focus primarily on how to apply a filter to a capture after it has been running to sort out unwanted data. An example of a capture that needs filtering is shown in Figure 6.1.

There are multiple ways you can go about filtering for data; however, since this is a field guide there is an important step you should take prior to applying any filter. Before you consider a filter, first consider why you need any filtering in particular so that you can assess which filter you need to build and apply. Here is an example:

1. You get a report that you believe a problem exists on a network where you may need to do protocol analysis in order to solve it. You first ask specific questions so that you know where you need to place Wireshark in order to capture this relevant data. The problem is reported that an Apple wireless device cannot connect to the network.

2. You find a network device in which you can mirror a port and collect SPAN data from a Cisco switchport to collect the relevant data needed to solve the problem into Wireshark.

3. You collect 30 minutes worth of capture data and save it to your disk in a capture file. You revisit the capture file and open it to inspect and analyze it. You want to narrow down what you are

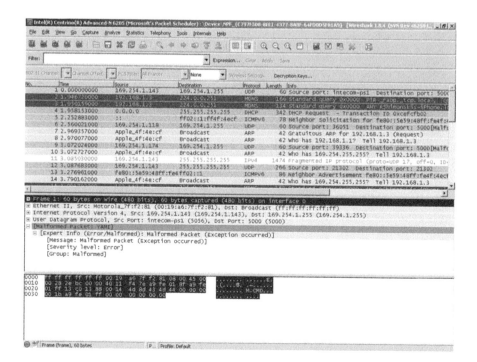

Figure 6.1 The Wireshark capture window.

looking for, so you can either filter by IP address (suspect system) and/or protocol used (Apple-based).

This is what needs to be done before you place Wireshark in a location to collect the data, prior to collecting data and essentially before doing any filtering or analysis of said data. You will then want to look for the problems by filtering out any data that is not relevant to the problem and inspecting the data that is relevant.

So, how do we apply a filter? The most basic way to apply a filter is by typing it into the filter box at the top of the Wireshark capture window and clicking Apply (or pressing Enter). For example, type "arp" and you can only view ARP packets. When you start typing, Wireshark will help you autocomplete your filter and you may not have to click on Apply; however, to remove the filter, you need to click on Clear. You can Save the filter by clicking on Save. In the example in Figure 6.2, we were able to narrow down that we have multiple devices using Address Resolution Protocol (ARP) broadcasting on the network segment.

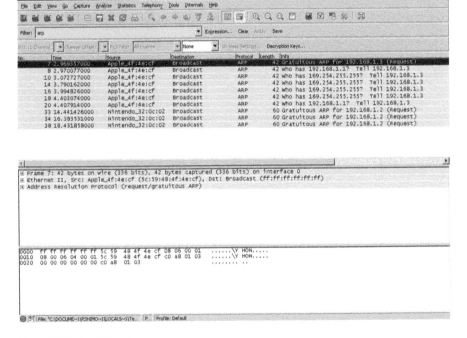

Figure 6.2 Viewing ARP packets.

In this example, we were able to narrow down our view of the problem area and quickly isolate relevant data that maybe part of the problem.

6.3 ADVANCED FILTER CREATION

In some cases you can always create a filter by using the Wireshark Filter Expression dialog box as shown in Figure 6.3. By doing so, you can get into more advanced level filter creation techniques such as picking a Filter name, its Relation, Value, Predefined values, and Range as seen in Figure 6.3. You can find the Expression Filter by clicking on the Expression link next to the Filter field in the Wireshark capture window.

●●●———————————————————————————

Using the advanced filters you build in the expression filter teach you how to write out advanced filter strings in the Wireshark capture window Filter field. Once you create enough filters, you will learn how to type them directly into the Filter field. By using autocomplete, you can speed up your ability to quickly build and apply filters and search for relevant data.

Another advanced level tip you can apply when creating filters is to simply let autocomplete assist you in your journey. In Figure 6.4, you can see an example of autocomplete in use. In this example, if you want to search for an arp filter, simply type the letter "a" into the field and a dropdown box will appear showing you all options starting with "a" (arp included). You can further develop this by learning the

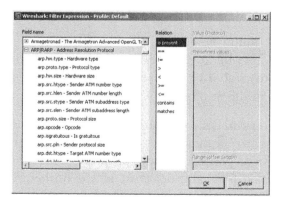

Figure 6.3 The Wireshark Filter Expression dialog box.

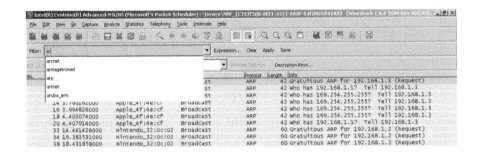

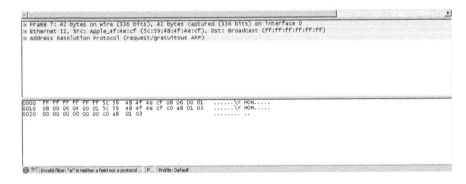

Figure 6.4 Using autocomplete.

Boolean arguments and they will also appear in the Filter field as well as ranges and so on.

You can also click the Analyze menu and select Display Filters to create a new filter.

6.4 OTHER FILTERING TECHNIQUES

Once you have built a number of filters and applied them to captured data, you can also build capture filters by clicking on the Analyze menu where a myriad of options will present themselves—all of which will be covered in this section.

By clicking on Analyze, you can select Display Filters and you will open the Wireshark Capture Filter dialog box as shown in Figure 6.5. In this dialog box, you can click on New to create a new filter, or select a predefined filter and delete or edit it further. This is a quick way to access the most commonly used filters used to solve problems today. Most problems result in IP, ARP, TCP, HTTP, and other

Figure 6.5 The Wireshark Capture Filter dialog box.

commonly used protocols on networks. If you click on the Capture Filter field in Figure 6.5 and look at the Properties fields, you can see exactly how the filter is created.

You can also Add the Filter name and Filter string data and click on New to add the filter you just created to the Display Filter field.

In Chapter 3, we learnt how to apply filters to the profile default prior to opening and running an actual capture in the Wireshark capture window. The Wireshark Capture Filter dialog box discussed here is identical to that same filter discussed in Chapter 3.

Another helpful tip to set up filter expressions is to go into the Wireshark capture window menu system. Under Analyze select Display Filter Macros. You can build a complete macro set to apply when you select filters. For those of you have done C programming in the past, macros are basically creating a function with one or more variables. Yet another way to build filter expressions to be added to the predefined set is to go into Wireshark Preferences in the Edit menu. This will open the dialog box as shown in Figure 6.6.

In the Filter Expressions menu option, you can click on Add and build a new filter expression as well as enable and disable it as needed.

6.5 CUSTOMIZED FILTERING AND TROUBLESHOOTING

In the previous sections, we covered the basic configuration of creating and applying filters to captured traffic in hopes that by doing so it will

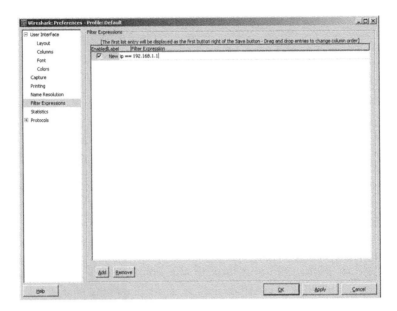

Figure 6.6 Setting Filter Expressions in preferences.

be easier and quicker for you as a technician to solve network problems. That being said, let us take a deeper dive into filter creation to troubleshoot common problems. In Figure 6.7, we will analyze a TCP-based conversation to assess it for problems.

In this example, we can select a packet in the Wireshark capture window and apply a filter directly to that packet. By right clicking on a particular packet you can produce a menu as seen in Figure 6.7, where you can apply as a Filter, set up a Conversation Filter, apply a Color Filter, or follow streams. We have already focused on applying specific filters, so for this example we will learn how to follow streams.

The next logical questions that may come to mind are what is a traffic stream and why would we want to filter it out? The answers are simple. The stream dialog window as seen in Figure 6.8 is going to filter out the Application layer details and show you what they are. In Chapter 1, we covered the OSI model which is extremely important in the field of networking to understand. The top layer which is the Application layer is at times very important to analyze when troubleshooting a problem. For example, let us say we had a problem to solve that resulted in a web browser having issues accessing a Web page. We would want to inspect HTTP traffic.

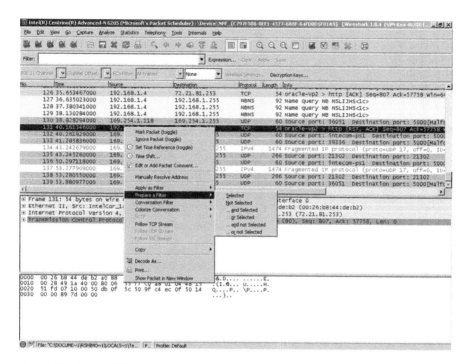

Figure 6.7 Configuring a filter on TCP traffic.

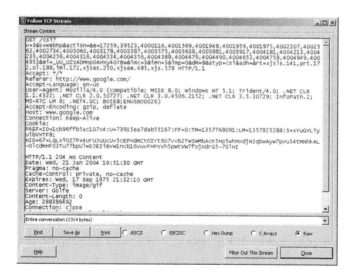

Figure 6.8 Following a TCP stream.

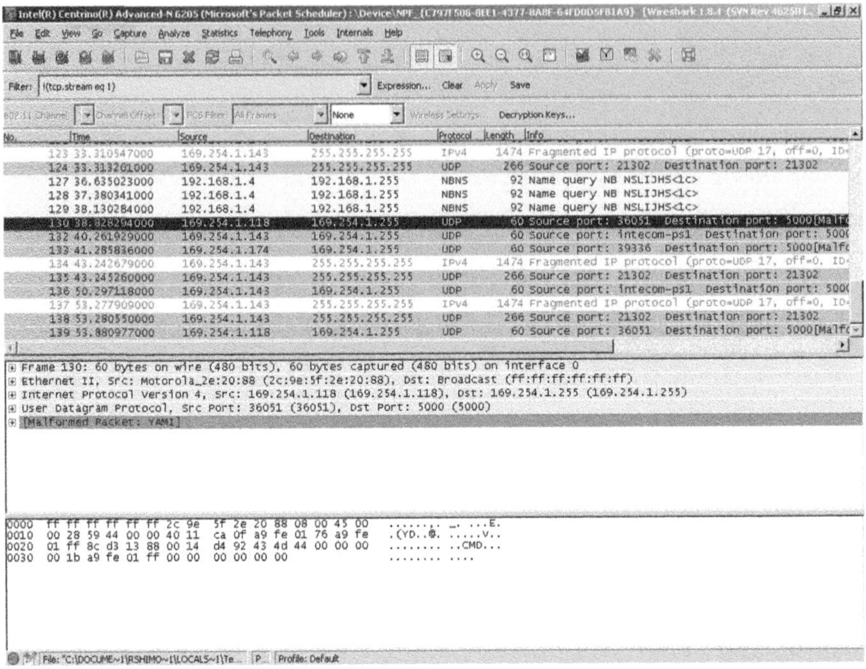

Figure 6.9 Applying a TCP stream filter in the Filter Field.

The application stream would be from the TCP-based IP address and the Details pane could show you the specifics of HTTP, however too really filter and see the HTTP traffic, you would need to apply the stream filter. In Figure 6.8, we can see the specifics of the communication with the web server and the interaction with the web browser.

You could also apply this type of filter directly into the Filter field in the Wireshark capture window as shown in Figure 6.9.

You could type the following into the Filter field to get the same result:

tcp.stream eq 1

You can also apply UDP stream filters as shown in Figure 6.10, where the Follow UDP Stream dialog box shows the UDP protocol specifics we want to analyze at the Application layer.

Here in this conversation we can see XML-based information showing how UDP is interacting at the Application layer. In this particular

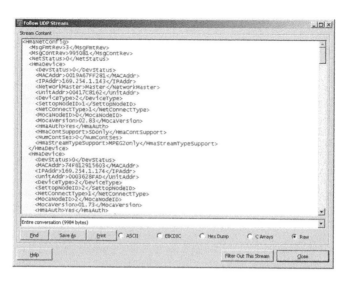

Figure 6.10 Follow UDP stream.

stream, we can see that there may be an issue with the Microsoft defined Automatic Private IP Addressing (APIPA) where a host cannot communicate with other hosts on the same range.

In Figure 6.11, we can see the application of a stream filter in the Filter field of the Wireshark capture window. Here we see that APIPA while being used via UDP can be further filtered out for analysis.

You could type the following into the Filter field to get the same result:

(ip.addr eq 169.254.1.143 and ip.addr eq 255.255.255.255) and (udp.port eq 21302 and udp.port eq 21302)

It should be mentioned that this does not mean that you will immediately be able to diagnose a problem with this information, remember that Wireshark helps you uncover the data in packets so you can attempt to isolate and resolve problems, Wireshark does not necessarily point out problems to you, you have to understand and know what you are looking for.

In this example, we would have a computer that does not communicate on the network using a specific IP address. We could go to that workstation and open a command prompt, type in ipconfig/all and find that the computer is in fact using an automatically configured IP

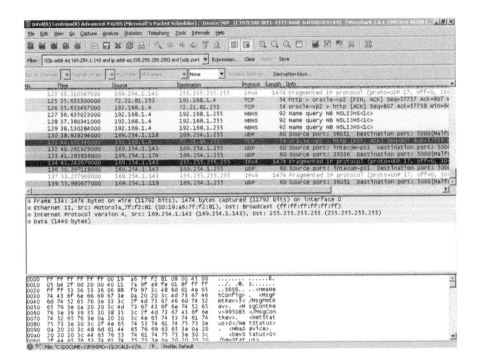

Figure 6.11 Filtering a UDP stream on an APIPA range.

address with APIPA. Is the computer not able to communicate with a DHCP server thus not able to get a dynamically assigned IP in order to communicate? Should the workstation be statically assigned? Furthermore, can we ping other hosts on the APIPA range? Is this how the workstation is supposed to be set up?

When troubleshooting problems, it is important to remember what we covered before in this book—you need to use Wireshark as a tool to augment other tools and your knowledge; otherwise, it may not specifically point you in the right direction.

6.6 CONVERSATION FILTERS

Lastly, we will cover building conversation filters. This can be done by right clicking on a specific packet conversation between source and destination address and select Conversation Filter, then for this example select IP. An example of this can be seen in Figure 6.12.

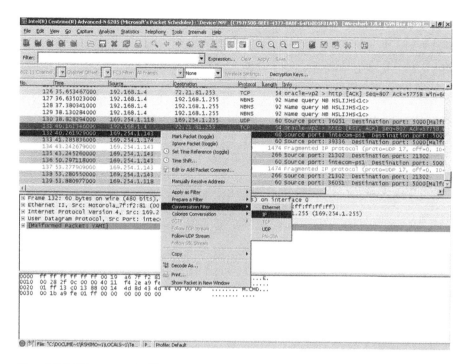

Figure 6.12 Building conversation filters.

Conversation filters are important when you want to troubleshoot communications between two specific hosts on a network. Here is a scenario in which you will want to build a conversation filter. Let us say you have a computer on your network (source) communicating with another computer (destination) and performance is somewhat slow. You may want to inspect the entire conversation between these two hosts carefully and look for clues on what may be the delay by looking at what the conversation consists of, using timestamps to see how long specific transmissions take place, when using TCP if the traffic goes through the three-way handshake of SYN−SYN, ACK−ACK, and many other examples.

In this example, we simply want to look at the basics of IP and by doing so we can uncover these problems. Here we see that the timing between the hosts are in milliseconds and that there are no clues given as to what could be happening in the conversation to cause an issue. That does not mean there is no issue, nor does it mean that Wireshark proved entirely that it is not a network issue; it just got you closer to ruling out what may not be impacting this conversation. In this

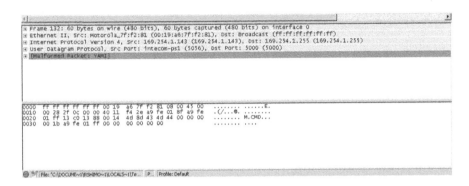

Figure 6.13 Filtering out an IP conversation via UDP.

example, the hosts are communicating without issue; however, the problem is that the network switch got disconnected from the gateway where the DHCP server was sitting and the hosts moved to the APIPA range therefore they are not able to communicate with a specific application; however, more filtering and analysis need to take place to determine why.

In Figure 6.13, we can use the Details pane of the Wireshark capture window to uncover malformed packets when UDP/IP conversations are built via Wireshark.

You could type the following into the Filter field to get the same result:

ip.addr eq 169.254.1.143 and ip.addr eq 169.254.1.255

In this example and previous examples in the chapter, the specifics of building filters to concisely list out what it is you need to look at (relevant data). There are literally hundreds if not thousands of examples that can be given depending on what the problem is, how big your network is, how many systems are being used, and so on. Remember, it takes time to learn how to build filters so hopefully this field guide gave you enough to get you started on your journey. Make sure you visit the Wireshark wiki as well as other sources of information to learn more.

6.7 SUMMARY

In this chapter, we learnt about filtering captured data in hopes to give you the ability to analyze and troubleshoot your problems by streamlining the data you will view and find relevant. As you can see from the last two chapters, filtering data can be done in many ways and in some ways can be confusing if you do not know what you are essentially looking for so understanding the problem at a high level is important to the process. In the next chapter, we will look at sample captures and apply some of these filtering techniques we learnt thus far. This will set us up for Chapter 8 where we will start inspecting packets for problems, looking into the headers, and learning about the deeper analysis we need to do to solve problems.

Sample Captures

In the previous six chapters of this field guide, we have explored the fundamental steps of getting Wireshark downloaded, installed, and prepped for use. We have explored common problems and looked at how to get up and running quickly with this packet capture and analysis tool. In the last three chapters, we have looked at how to capture and filter data as well as the common problems associated with why you would need to use Wireshark in the first place. We have gone through troubleshooting methodologies and given you an understanding of why knowing when to use Wireshark is essential to using it effectively. We have also learned tips on how to capture and filter relevant data.

In this chapter, we will learn more about captured data as we explore sample captures and discuss problems that can be solved with Wireshark in conjunction with the situation presented. For example, if you had a Dynamic Host Configuration Protocol (DHCP) problem, what exactly would you do to set Wireshark up to help you isolate the problem? What exactly does the tool offer you to help baseline what the problem may be? Let us review a sample capture and find out.

This chapter of the field guide covers a few basic problems and focuses on methodology, which is one of the most important aspects to learn when trying to master Wireshark. Review each problem in its entirety in order to benefit from each example.

7.1 GETTING STARTED

In this chapter, we expand on what we learned in Chapter 6 by covering some advanced problems, how to solve them using Wireshark, and the more complex use of analysis by applying more filters and reviewing expert analysis reports. Your learning of Wireshark can be augmented by real-world examples, which we will cover here. You can run your own captures and filter for relevant data, or you can download the sample captures highlighted within the chapter. You can also use this chapter as a way to build a methodology you can use each time you are presented with a new problem. No matter how you approach each issue, remember that methodology is the key to unlocking your answers to root cause.

7.2 SAMPLE CAPTURES

Sample captures can be downloaded online. We will start with using a predownloaded capture file so that you can learn the methodology. To view capture samples on the Wireshark Wiki, simply open the Wireshark tool, and on the landing page, click on Sample Captures. Here, you will find approximately 100 samples of previously captured data that you can review. This is an excellent way to help bolster your knowledge on packet capture and analysis and network protocols. For example, you can review the many different protocols used on networks today if you are not an expert in protocol analysis and can perform this function everyday. You can also capture and filter your own data if you prefer.

●●●————————————————————————————————————

You can find and review captured data on the Wireshark Wiki. You can find the data to review in the following pages:

http://wiki.wireshark.org/SampleCaptures
http://wiki.wireshark.org/CaptureFilters

You can contribute to the capture sample repository by going to the sample captures page and following the instructions listed on the main page. It will explain the correct process and format for you to follow so that you can contribute.

In this example, we will look at the DHCP, which is an extremely common protocol used today. DHCP is used to dynamically assign IP addresses to systems that request them so they can connect to and communicate on a network. What you may know already is how the basic architecture of DHCP is laid out; however, you may or may not know the specifics of the underlying functions of the protocol and what may go wrong. You would use Wireshark to determine this.

Figure 7.1 shows the basic architecture that would be needed for DHCP clients to get dynamically assigned addressing from a DHCP server. Here, we have put the clients on one subnet and the server on a separate subnet. We have added a firewall as well.

How is it supposed to work?

1. DHCP clients will communicate with a server using UDP port 67 to send data to the DHCP server, and UDP port 68 to send data to the DHCP client.

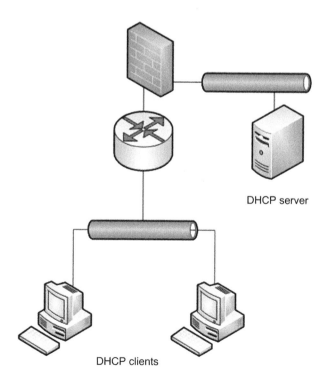

DHCP server

DHCP clients

Figure 7.1 Understanding how DHCP works.

2. Since DHCP communicates via UDP, they can communicate on the same subnet without issue; however, if moving across a router to a separate subnet, a DHCP relay will be needed to forward the communications to the DHCP server for communication to take place.
3. Once the path has been verified and communication is possible, the clients and the server communicate via a process called DORA: Discovery, Offer, Request, and Acknowledgment.
4. A discovery packet is sent from the client to the server. The server then makes an IP lease offer. The client then makes an IP request, and the server acknowledges with an IP lease.

As you can see, there are many things that could go wrong and many reasons why it would be important to perhaps set up a port mirror (or Wireshark on the host directly) to solve this issue. You can also set up Wireshark directly on the DHCP server or the clients.

●●●───

You can find more information on protocols, ports, and address assignments by visiting this site: http://www.iana.org/assignments/service-names-port-numbers/service-names-port-numbers.xml.

───

To see this in Wireshark, you would need to capture the client (source) communicating with the DHCP server (destination) and filter for DHCP. This is shown in Figure 7.2.

Here, we can see how the communication takes place between the client, to the server, back to the client and then finally with the server responding back to the client with an acknowledgment and IP lease.

In Wireshark, we can see the specifics of this communication and could quite potentially verify its taking place and/or find where the problems may be taking place. Here are some examples:

1. If the DHCP relay agent (a Cisco IP Helper Address commonly found on Cisco devices) is not configured properly (or at all), you will not see a communication back from the server.
2. If a firewall in place does not allow for the DHCP protocol to communicate bidirectional, it will be blocked.
3. If the clients are sending discovery packets to an IP address, but a rogue DHCP server exists, we can find those packets in the trace.

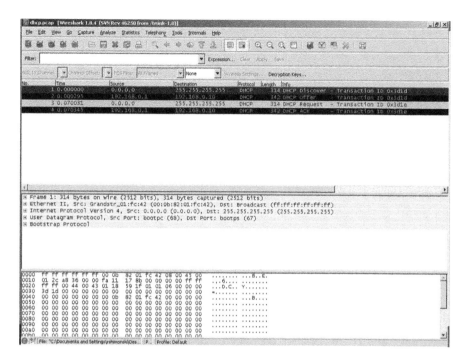

Figure 7.2 Viewing DHCP traffic in Wireshark.

4. If the clients have a firewall configured locally, we can see that the discovery packets are not getting to the port mirror configured to capture the traffic.

This is one example of how Wireshark can help you see the details of what may be causing a network issue, specifically with dynamic assignment of IP addresses. We can even look deeper into the data to solve problems.

DHCP works by using BOOTP, also known as the Bootstrap Protocol. In the Wireshark capture window, you can view the Discover data by highlighting that specific frame and expanding the Detail pane's view and scrolling down to the BOOTP data. This is shown in Figure 7.3.

Here, we can isolate specific data. Specifically, we can see that the data is sent unicast and contains no relevant IP addressing data until the full DORA process takes place. By jumping ahead and reviewing the final IP lease information provided by the DHCP server, you can

Figure 7.3 Viewing DHCP discover in Wireshark.

see that an IP address has been given to the client for use: 192.168.0.10. This is shown in Figure 7.4.

This is only one simple example that you can view to understand why methodology and knowledge of architecture and basic protocol will help you solve problems using Wireshark. Without knowing the layout of the systems, which can come from discovery or already drawn up maps, you will have a hard time isolating what the problem may be or where it may be coming from.

Having basic knowledge of protocols is also important for you to successfully troubleshoot the Wireshark. Without knowing that DHCP functions a certain way, using certain ports and underlying protocols, you will have a hard time isolating a break in the system with Wireshark.

7.3 EXPERT ANALYSIS

A commonly used tool with Wireshark is called Expert Info. It can help you diagnose serious problems, or sometimes point you to a problem that does not really exist. This is called a "false positive."

As we mentioned in Chapter 1, Wireshark is a tool that requires you to understand the basics of networking, know how computer

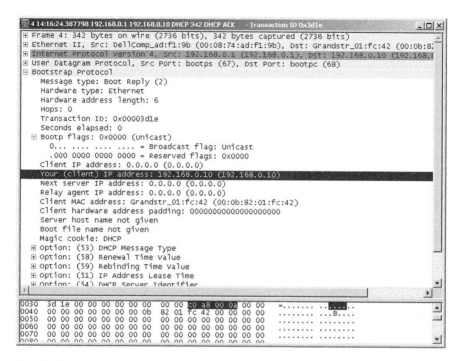

Figure 7.4 Viewing DHCP acknowledgment in Wireshark.

systems operate, and even know details down into the hardware, software, and NIC card drivers.

This is where troubleshooting can get tricky. In Figure 7.5, the Wireshark Expert Info is shown. This can be invoked by going to the Analyze menu in the Wireshark capture window and selecting Expert Info from the drop down menu. Here, you can view the Errors, Warnings, Notes, Chats, Details, and Packet Comments tabs.

Each tab provides specific data you can use to learn more about your current capture data and get clues on possible issues. For example, in these tabs, you may find that these are malformed packets as shown in Figure 7.5. Commonly found problems are malformed packets, checksum errors, out-of-order packets, Transmission Control Protocol (TCP) retransmissions, resets, and duplicate acknowledgments, to name a few.

In each section, you can find specific details on what Wireshark has analyzed from the captured data. What the Expert Info does is

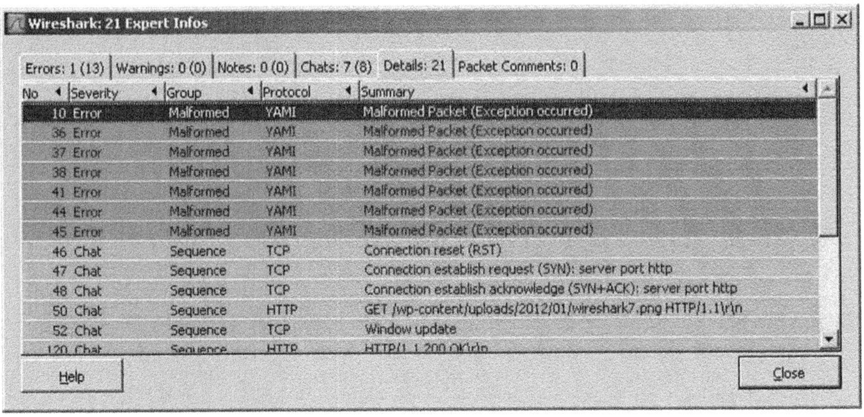

Figure 7.5 Viewing Expert Info in Wireshark.

correlate the entire capture and come up with some basic assumptions of what is taking place on the network. For example, in Figure 7.5, Wireshark has found a series of malformed packets that you would have had to scan through each packet in the Details pane to find.

As we reviewed earlier in the chapter with the DHCP acknowledge packet in the DORA process, we found an error in the packet as shown in Figure 7.6.

What this means is simple; there is a calculated error found on the data that Wireshark captured and Wireshark flagged this data as "bad." This does not necessarily mean that you have a problem, however. What this could mean in this sequence of packets is that the checksum may not have been calculated prior to Wireshark capturing the data.

> To troubleshoot TCP problems with a high degree of success, you will need to understand how TCP is a connection-based technology and UDP is connectionless. Understanding how the three-way-handshake works and the inner workings of TCP is critical to solving problems in regards to communications on data networks. We will learn more about the three-way-handshake in Chapter 8.

It can be confusing to some to see an error and find that it is not always an error, but how the system works with Wireshark, hence why

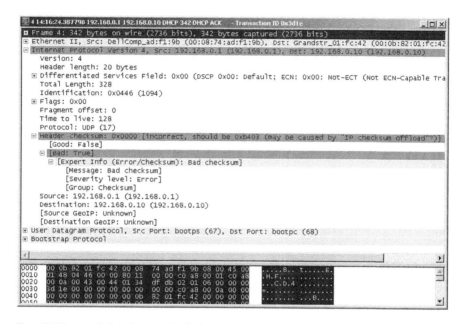

Figure 7.6 Viewing a bad checksum in Wireshark.

they call it a false positive. The checksum is in fact bad to Wireshark; however, because it was captured before it was calculated simply means that it could possibly be ok. A good way to root out false positives is by looking at the Expert Info window's "other" problems taking place at the same time. If there are dozens of retransmissions, out-of-order packets, and so on, it means, it is possible that the bad checksum may also be relevant. Figure 7.7 shows an example of a bad checksum problem where no other problems exist, ruling that it could possibly be a false positive.

●●●

A quick way to find a problematic packet is to open the Expert Info dialog box and click on the error message in the tabs. This will direct you to the problem packet in the Wireshark capture window Summary pane.

7.4 FLOW GRAPHS

Another commonly used tool with Wireshark is a flow graph. A flow graph can be used to find details about all messages used in a stream. We learned about TCP and UDP streams and what they can provide. In a flow graph, you can show all of them (or sections of them) in a reportable graph tool. By opening the Wireshark capture window and

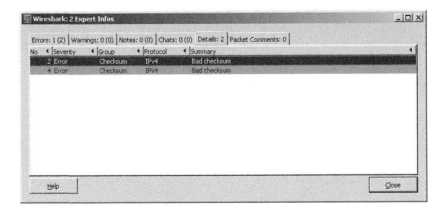

Figure 7.7 Viewing a bad checksum in Wireshark.

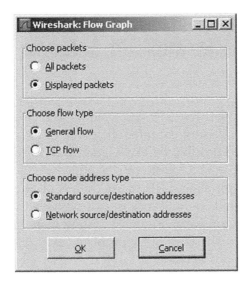

Figure 7.8 Viewing a flow graph in Wireshark.

clicking on the Statistics menu, you will find Flow Graph. Select it, and open the Wireshark Flow Graph dialog box as shown in Figure 7.8

Here, we want to view the TCP-based communications in the current capture to see what types of queries are taking place. In Figure 7.9, the specific output from the Flow Graph is shown. Here, we see the Time window which is set to show us specifically each TCP steam taking place at that time, from source to destination.

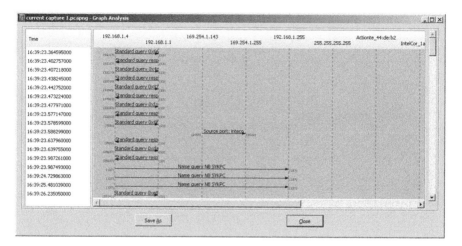

Figure 7.9 Viewing a flow graph in Wireshark.

If you click on one of the arrows/flows within the graph, it will highlight the relevant packet in the main window.

Flow graphs help in seeing how the traffic on the network looks like as a whole, not just from single source and destination pairs. You can see how many hosts are having conversations with a single host and then can find out if that host may or may not be overwhelmed with connections.

You may have to adjust the time-stamping options in order to specifically report on time. In order to do this, open the Wireshark capture window and click on the View menu, select Time Display Format, and then adjust the time settings you would like to see, which is shown in Figure 7.10.

To learn more about specific problems, a great place to learn from, discuss with all levels of expertise, and ask questions is the Wireshark Ask forum.

http://ask.wireshark.org

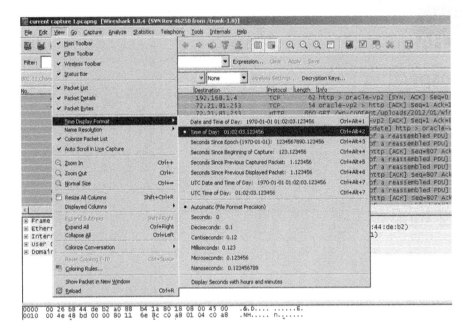

Figure 7.10 Adjusting time in Wireshark.

7.5 SUMMARY

In this chapter, we have learned more about how to solve problems with captured and filtered data. So far, we have learned how to get Wireshark up and running and use it to capture data and filter it; however, we have now expanded into topics that show the real power of Wireshark and what it can help you discover. In Chapter 8, we will look under the hood and learn how to conduct more detailed analysis with Wireshark.

Inspecting Packets

In this chapter, we will learn how to use Wireshark to inspect packets and isolate network and system problems. In this chapter, we will look at a single problem and show you how deeply you can dive into the data that is captured by Wireshark for your analysis. We will cover the inspection of a problem posed on a switched Ethernet network, very common in today's environments where bridging loops create storms that impact the network in adversely.

In this chapter's example, we will cover a spanning tree protocol (STP) issue and go deeper into packet analysis and what Wireshark can do, show you, and help you analyze in hopes to solve a problem.

> Make sure that if you are encouraged to test any of the theories in this chapter, you do it on a test network. Spanning tree loops and the packet storms that follow it can cripple your network to the point where it cannot be used.

8.1 GETTING STARTED

As we learn more about Wireshark, we will discuss problems found on a network and specifically why they occur from the packet level. Here we will take an in depth look at a few common (and not so common) problems and what you are looking for in the packets, how to use the tool to get and view this information and how to use Wireshark to solve them. We will also look at other tools you can use to augment the use of Wireshark to solve complex network and system issues.

8.2 UNDERSTANDING THE TECHNOLOGY

STP is a network technology that helps logically manage a switched (or bridged) network that has redundant connections so that you do not have "loops" in the network topology. It is a protocol that runs on the network switches and can be configured to be optimized, however, it is generally operational by default. STP (which we will call Spanning Tree for short ongoing) is an IEEE standard. It is known by the identifier 802.1D.

The way it works is simple. It will allow data to traverse on one connection, but will block the redundant connection to prevent a loop, which in turn can cause a broadcast storm that floods the network with packets and causes all devices to process this data at a rapid rate thereby causing other symptoms, such as high CPU and I/O use. When Spanning Tree is put in place, it can keep a network very stable and it recommended whenever you have more than one connection to any single device. A Spanning Tree is created by the switches on the network and can be configured.

A device called a root bridge (usually the system with the lowest bridge ID computed by a priority number, a port number, and a MAC address) maintains the Spanning Tree for that particular network segment.

Figure 8.1 shows an example of a very simple network hierarchy where five network switches are connected together to form a LAN.

In Figure 8.1, we see ports (where connecting links uplink to other switches) configured in a way where data can traverse the network without creating a loop. The root port (RP) forwards the data based on a computation of least cost path from the switch in which it is connected. The designated port (DP) is the least cost path for that segment that connects each switch. This creates the least cost path. However, if a loop is present from a redundant port, that port is put into a blocked state and becomes a blocked port (BP).

When the Spanning Tree is configured, running and optimal and all ports are stable as well the Spanning Tree is considered "converged."

Ports become a RP, DP, or BP by going through a series of states. When a connection is made to a switch the port (through Spanning

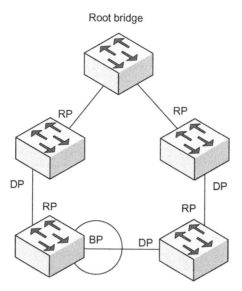

Root bridge

Figure 8.1 Typical network with STP.

Tree) will go through the process of listening, learning, forwarding, blocking, or disabling. These are explained as follows:

1. Listening: When a port is listening, it does not pass traffic. It does not populate the MAC address table where the switch makes its switching decisions.
2. Learning: When a port is learning, it does not pass traffic. It does populate the MAC address table where the switch makes its switching decisions.
3. Forwarding: When a port is forwarding, it is sending traffic based on the MAC address table where the switch makes its switching decisions.
4. Blocking: If a port is identified as a potential for a loop, the port is put into blocking state. This does not disable the port, it only blocks traffic to and from it. The reason why this is important is because when you want redundancy this port becomes part of the redundancy. For example, you may have a switch to fail over to another switch if it fails. If one switch fails, the BP switches to forwarding and data continues to flow through the network.
5. Disabling: Normally a port is in disabling state when it is manually shutdown or disconnected completely.

●●●——————————————————————————————

It is recommended that you use rapid spanning tree protocol (RSTP) IEEE 802.1w to limit the default timers used in order to reach convergence. RSTP uses roles, such as root, designated, alternate, backup, and disabled. It ports the port states learning, forwarding, and discarding.

——————————————————————————————

The states in which the Spanning Tree transform into and how it maintains convergence is done by information sent to and from each switch through bridge protocol data units (BPDUs).

A BPDU is the data that traverses the Spanning Tree topology devices through the network to control how the Spanning Tree operates. When using Wireshark, this is specifically what you will capture in order to troubleshoot Spanning Tree problems. A BPDU frame is broken down into 12 fields as shown in Figure 8.2.

These fields will become relevant when you start to capture Spanning Tree data and review within the Wireshark capture window.

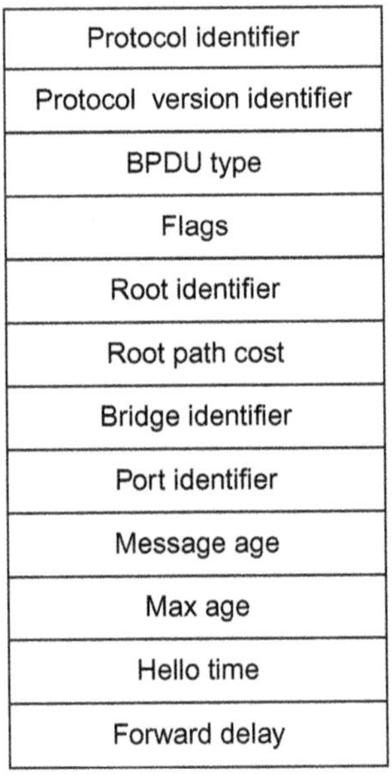

Protocol identifier
Protocol version identifier
BPDU type
Flags
Root identifier
Root path cost
Bridge identifier
Port identifier
Message age
Max age
Hello time
Forward delay

Figure 8.2 BPDU fields.

8.3 CAPTURING AND FILTERING DATA

Now that we understand how a Spanning Tree is supposed to operate, let's look at some common problems that may occur within it and why when capturing data with Wireshark is equally important to understand. Some common problems you may encounter are (but not limited to):

- Spanning Tree 802.1D used instead of 802.1w
- No root bridge configured or a root bridge configured on an under-powered device not centered in your topology
- Using redundancy [with protocols such as Cisco's hot standby router protocol (HSRP)] and designing Spanning Tree incorrectly when using it
- Too many redundant links in a blocking state
- Not using STP or any other technology of its kind.

In this example, we connected to a switch in the core of the network closest to the center of the topology. Spanning Tree when captured by Wireshark can be filtered by using the Expression Filter as shown in Figure 8.3. As you review the filter expressions, it should clear that everything we just learned about is something you could filter for within the captured data you collect. In this example, we will look for the location of the root bridge using the captured BPDU frames.

Once we filter the data, we can see the root bridge captured in Figure 8.4. In this example, we filtered for the STP. BPDUs sent through the network every 2 seconds are sent via a multicast address. The address is 01:80:C2:00:00:00.

To do a deep dive of this, we need to select a frame with this multicast address and filter deeper for the root bridge. We can then move from the Summary pane into the Detail pane as shown in Figure 8.5.

The root bridge can be found within the sections of the Details pane, which we will dig into next.

8.4 INSPECTION OF THE DATA

Now that we have captured and filtered for the relevant data, we are now ready to do a deeper inspect of the data within the frame. We need to recall the BPDU frame we learned about in Figure 8.2. In the

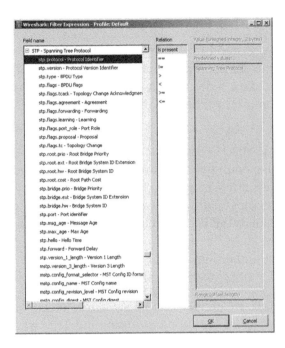

Figure 8.3 Filtering STP.

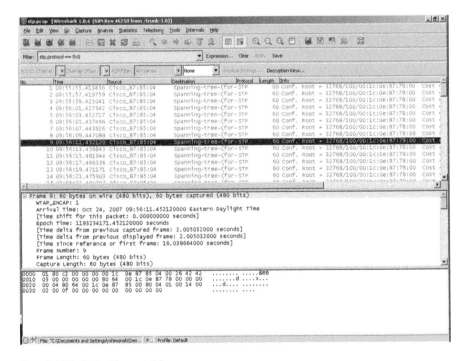

Figure 8.4 Wireshark with captured data.

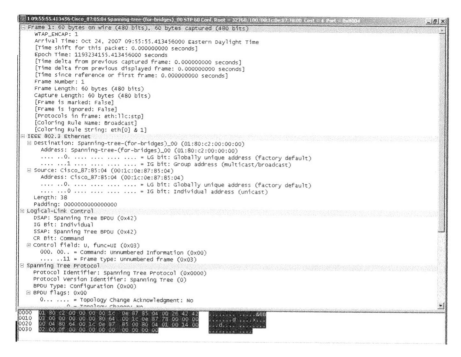

Figure 8.5 Searching for the root bridge in the Detail pane.

Details pane, we can review the specifics we learned about such as first reviewing the Frame field as shown in Figure 8.6. Here we can review when the frame was captured and its size.

Next, we can review the Ethernet field as shown in Figure 8.7. Here we can review the source and destination MAC address. We can see in the destination section the multicast address 01:80:C2:00:00:00. We can see the source MAC address comes from a Cisco switch.

Once we have found where the frame is coming from and where it is going to, we can inspect the LLC field. In Chapter 1, we reviewed the OSI model and learned that at layer 2 of the model we see its split into two layers, one being the LLC. When frames operate at layer 2 (using MAC addresses), the LLC field maintains specific data at a higher level in the model. In Figure 8.8, we can see that data as the BPDU information.

Once we have reviewed that data, we can see in the STP field (as shown in Figure 8.9) the specifics we were looking for, primarily the root bridge assignment as well as the MAC address associated with it.

```
⊟ Frame 1: 60 bytes on wire (480 bits), 60 bytes captured (480 bits)
    WTAP_ENCAP: 1
    Arrival Time: Oct 24, 2007 09:55:55.413456000 Eastern Daylight Time
    [Time shift for this packet: 0.000000000 seconds]
    Epoch Time: 1193234155.413456000 seconds
    [Time delta from previous captured frame: 0.000000000 seconds]
    [Time delta from previous displayed frame: 0.000000000 seconds]
    [Time since reference or first frame: 0.000000000 seconds]
    Frame Number: 1
    Frame Length: 60 bytes (480 bits)
    Capture Length: 60 bytes (480 bits)
    [Frame is marked: False]
    [Frame is ignored: False]
    [Protocols in frame: eth:llc:stp]
    [Coloring Rule Name: Broadcast]
    [Coloring Rule String: eth[0] & 1]
```

Figure 8.6 Inspecting the frame field.

```
⊟ IEEE 802.3 Ethernet
  ⊟ Destination: Spanning-tree-(for-bridges)_00 (01:80:c2:00:00:00)
      Address: Spanning-tree-(for-bridges)_00 (01:80:c2:00:00:00)
      .... ..0. .... .... .... .... = LG bit: Globally unique address (factory default)
      .... ...1 .... .... .... .... = IG bit: Group address (multicast/broadcast)
  ⊟ Source: Cisco_87:85:04 (00:1c:0e:87:85:04)
      Address: Cisco_87:85:04 (00:1c:0e:87:85:04)
      .... ..0. .... .... .... .... = LG bit: Globally unique address (factory default)
      .... ...0 .... .... .... .... = IG bit: Individual address (unicast)
    Length: 38
    Padding: 0000000000000000
```

Figure 8.7 Inspecting the Ethernet field.

```
    ⊟ Logical-Link Control
        DSAP: Spanning Tree BPDU (0x42)
        IG Bit: Individual
        SSAP: Spanning Tree BPDU (0x42)
        CR Bit: Command
      ⊟ Control field: U, func=UI (0x03)
          000. 00.. = Command: Unnumbered Information (0x00)
          .... ..11 = Frame type: Unnumbered frame (0x03)
```

Figure 8.8 Inspecting the LLC field.

Now we know what system holds the identity of the root bridge. To find what device this is on your network, you can either look in the MAC address tables and find the relevant port, then map the ARP tables to IP addresses if a layer 3 assignment is given.

8.5 ANALYSIS TOOLS

To maintain a healthy Spanning Tree and be able to monitor its stability, you should consider not only designing it correctly, but also

```
⊟ Spanning Tree Protocol
    Protocol Identifier: Spanning Tree Protocol (0x0000)
    Protocol Version Identifier: Spanning Tree (0)
    BPDU Type: Configuration (0x00)
  ⊟ BPDU flags: 0x00
      0... .... = Topology Change Acknowledgment: No
      .... ...0 = Topology Change: No
  ⊟ Root Identifier: 32768 / 100 / 00:1c:0e:87:78:00
      Root Bridge Priority: 32768
      Root Bridge System ID Extension: 100
      Root Bridge System ID: 00:1c:0e:87:78:00
    Root Path Cost: 4
  ⊟ Bridge Identifier: 32768 / 100 / 00:1c:0e:87:85:00
      Bridge Priority: 32768
      Bridge System ID Extension: 100
      Bridge System ID: 00:1c:0e:87:85:00
    Port identifier: 0x8004
    Message Age: 1
    Max Age: 20
    Hello Time: 2
    Forward Delay: 15
```

Figure 8.9 Inspecting the STP field.

managing and monitoring it the best you can. There are tools available to help you to do this.

Two notable tools that can help you manage and monitor your Spanning Tree network is the SolarWinds (www.solarwinds.com) network monitoring tools or the Cisco (www.cisco.com) network monitoring tools called Cisco Prime.

Other technologies you can put into place are configurations, such as RootGuard, PortFast, UplinkFast, LoopGuard, BPDUGuard, BPDUFilter, and BackboneFast from Cisco, which help you to further manage the stability of your Spanning Tree network.

8.6 SUMMARY

In this chapter, we looked at the specific details you could find when inspecting packets using Wireshark. In the example given, we took a look at how understanding a technology like Spanning Tree is critical to the process before a capture is even taken. Then, understanding the topology and where to capture data from equally important to finding specifically what you are looking for. We then filtered the data to find what we needed and inspected the data closely to find what we were looking for. In the next chapter, we will look deeper into the data to find out ways Wireshark can assist you with finding more complex issues and how to use other tools to help find a problem's root cause.

Deep Analysis

In this chapter, we will learn how to use Wireshark to go deeper into inspecting packets and isolating network and system problems. In this chapter, we will expand on what we learned in the last chapter but look at other areas of the network and the systems in use so that you can learn more about how to troubleshoot with Wireshark to solve problems at a deeper level.

In this chapter, we take a deeper look into the data, the systems and the network in order to define and find root cause of problems as well as how to use Wireshark and other enterprise tools to solve issues that occur over WAN links, when using a softphone and to find security problems. We will learn about probes, taps, and how all of these tools can be used together to create a complete picture to help you not only understand why data traverses a network a certain way but also why it chooses specific paths, how it interacts with destination systems, and what could go wrong within those conversations. We will look at Voice over IP (VoIP) problems, malicious software issues, how intrusion detection/prevention, scanning, and many other services work on a network and how Wireshark can help you work with them when solving issues.

9.1 GETTING STARTED

When you work with a network or are directly responsible for it, you will often hear that there are problems with it. Some are common help desk requests from users who have problems remembering their system passwords, and others are calls from users who cannot login because their network cable got unplugged again. Although these are common problems, and annoying at times, they are easily fixed through a quick series of troubleshooting steps and usually require a simple solution. We learned about using a troubleshooting methodology throughout this entire field guide.

End users constantly call the help desk and complain about the network, they normally say that the network is too slow. On the complaint list is a steady flow of why the speed of their logins is slow, hanging or frozen applications, or timed-out sessions? Obviously, there could be a problem with network performance if the majority of your users call to complain, however, sometimes it is isolated to a single location, network segment, or even one or two users. Where do you begin to look for the source of this problem? With enterprise networks growing and connecting to other companies' networks increasingly rapidly, monitoring network performance can become a cumbersome task.

In this chapter, we look at how to initially isolate a problem, monitor the network's performance using tools like Wireshark, and then offer tips on how to correct the issues.

9.2 DEEP ANALYSIS

For our first discussion, we will look at how to analyze a connection request from a source system to a destination system and analyzing any problems that can occur in between. When connections are established using the TCP/IP protocol stack the "manager" of this effort is handled by the TCP.

Some of the problems that can occur to cause issues with TCP from functioning correctly is ports being blocked by a firewall, a faulty network connection (such as a NIC card or switch port), or misconfigured settings on network and system devices.

TCP handshake is how connection-oriented communication takes place. For connectionless UDP is used. When TCP is used (e.g., to

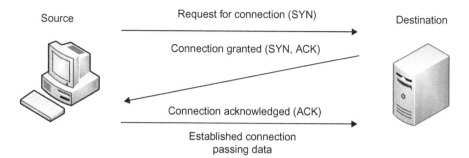

Figure 9.1 The TCP handshake sequence.

visit a website), TCP handles the connection establishment between the source and destination devices. When this connection establishment takes place, the first few packets sent back and forth are called the TCP handshake. How the TCP handshake works is shown in Figure 9.1. The source computer will request a connection to the destination by sending a packet with a SYN. This is usually initiated if you are going to use a resource on the server from the client such as requesting to view or use a web page as an example.

Once the request for connection has been made, the destination system (the server with the web page) will grant the connection with a SYN, ACK. Then the source system acknowledges the destination system with an ACK. Once the three-way handshake takes place, the connection is deemed established and data can pass. The result is that the source system (the client) can view the web page on the destination system (the server).

So now that we have an understanding on how TCP/IP works on your network, what would Wireshark show when you capture this communication between the source and destination? To view this communication, you need to capture data in between a source system and a destination and configure Wireshark to capture it. You can perform the same test by having a client connect to a web page on a server and capture the communication as seen in Figure 9.2.

As you can see in Figure 9.2, the client (192.168.1.4) is making a connect request to view a web page on a server (72.21.81.253). We have captured the communication as seen in the Wireshark capture window and it can be verified by looking in the Summary pane. Here you see the source and destination IP addresses as well as the protocols being used which are TCP and HTTP. This maps directly to our discussion and

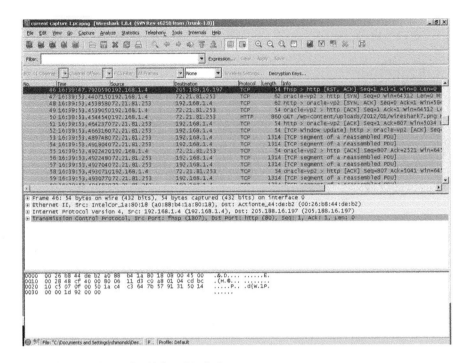

Figure 9.2 Viewing the TCP handshake in Wireshark.

example on a client visiting a web page on a server. You can use the Info section to derive the data such as the TCP handshake taking place.

So let us dive into reviewing the segments and review the finer details in the Details pane of Wireshark. In Figure 9.3, we have selected the first portion of the handshake to review. Here we see the client (source) sending a connection request to the server (destination) using port 80 (HTTP). In the flags field, we see the SYN bit set.

Once the connection is underway, the destination system needs to send a SYN, ACK back to the source as seen in Figure 9.4. In Figure 9.4, we can see the source IP address as the server and then destination switches to the client. We can see the flags set to SYN and ACK.

In Figure 9.5, we see the completion of the handshake by the source (client) sending an ACK to the destination (server) completing the handshake. In the flags section, we can see the ACK set.

When working with Wireshark to solve a network problem, you could attempt to capture this three-way handshake and check these

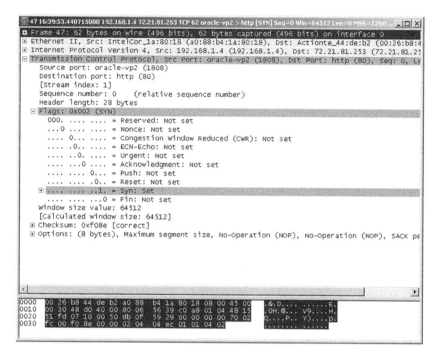

Figure 9.3 Viewing the TCP handshake in the Detail pane (SYN).

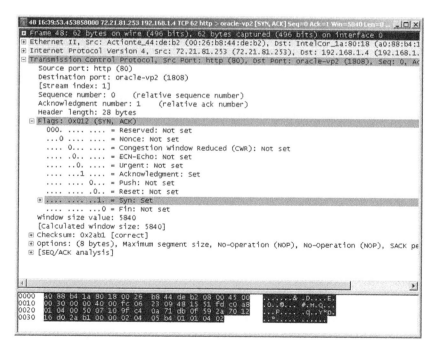

Figure 9.4 Viewing the TCP handshake in the Detail pane (SYN, ACK).

Figure 9.5 Viewing the TCP handshake in the Detail pane (ACK).

specific sections to see if, for example, the client sends a connection establishment request (SYN), and you do not see a SYN, ACK in return. Or, you can see disconnects in the established connection.

The flags are important because this is where you can see specific data in regards to what bits are actually turned on. TCP Windowing can also be seen in the flags section. Many applications rely on a network to be able to perform adequately and if there is a large amount of small packets, fragmentation, retransmissions, high buffering, or other problems associated with causing performance problems, you can use the data found in your captures to find and then resolve them.

In Figure 9.6, we can review the TCP windowing flag. TCP hosts when communicating need to agree to limit or amount of data that can be sent at any given time. This is called the TCP window size and found in the TCP header.

In this example, we can see that the window size has been configured to a predetermined (or agreed) size. This is determined on the initial SYN sent to establish the connection via the source system. In this

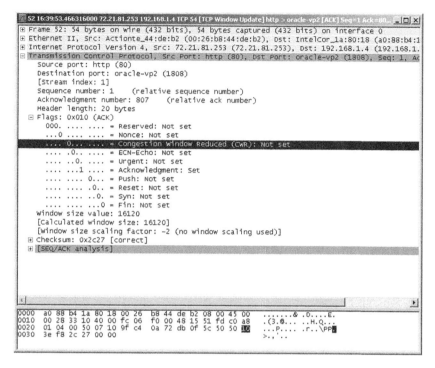

Figure 9.6 The TCP windowing process.

example, no scaling was used and the preset or predetermined sizing was used. If a problem did exist, you would see congestion notifications in use as seen in Figure 9.6.

Some Windows systems (such as Vista as an example) used autotuning features to adjust TCP flow. You can also find these types of issues when working with Wireshark by reviewing the details pane very closely and monitoring the specific sizing details noted earlier.

9.3 ANALYZING FLOW

There are other ways you can use Wireshark to review connections from source to destination. As we covered earlier in the field guide, using flow graphs can be a helpful way to review communications on your network. To set up a flow graph, go to the Wireshark capture window and select the Statistics menu and choose Flow Graph from the drop down menu. In Figure 9.7, you can configure the flow graph how you would like to see it. In this example, choose TCP flow.

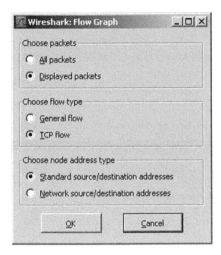

Figure 9.7 Configuring a flow graph.

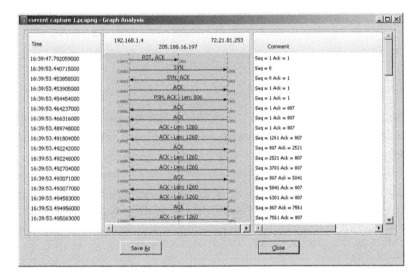

Figure 9.8 Viewing the TCP handshake in a flow graph.

In Figure 9.8, you can see the flow graph created around the previous example of the TCP handshake sequence. Here you can see specifically how long it took and what sequence numbers were being used. This is a quick way to see if you have latency issues where or problems with the sequence.

In sum, TCP communication is a critical component to TCP/IP network communication. It manages the established connection and ensures that the oriented connection remains established and data traverses the network from source to destination and if any problems occur, Wireshark can help find exactly what may have caused the issue when you review and analyze the captured and filtered data.

9.4 TROUBLESHOOTING PHONES

In this example, we will look at another problem and take a deep dive into how to solve it using Wireshark. Here we will look at how a softphone could have an issue connecting to a destination and how Wireshark can help assist you in finding out why.

In Figure 9.9, we use a simple softphone loaded on a Windows client to initiate a call to another host. In this example, we can see that the account failed to enable and the error given by the phone is that the network data needs to be verified. This is something that Wireshark should be able to uncover rather quickly.

Our next step would be to use Wireshark to capture the data from the source (the softphone) to the destination (the connecting host). In Figure 9.10, we see the data captured by Wireshark indicating that the phone is trying to register a connection to the connecting host. We can see the source and destination IP addresses as well as the protocol in use which is the session initiation protocol (SIP).

As we dig deeper into the Detail pane, we can see specific data that is relevant to solving the problem. In this case, a firewall was blocking the connection and causing the softphone to ring but no one is able to answer thus not being able to register to the unified communications system where it needs to register (Figure 9.11).

You can also review specific SIP statistics as seen in Figure 9.12 by going to the Wireshark capture window and selecting the Telephony menu, then selecting SIP. Once you select SIP you can click on Create Stat. You can then review the specific statistics such as how many packets were sent, resent, and specifically get an average baseline for how long it takes for calls to setup.

Figure 9.9 Using a network softphone.

9.5 SECURITY ANALYSIS

In our next example, we will look at how Wireshark can be used to identify security issues on your network. In this example, we have used sample captures found in the Wireshark online capture repository.

To take a deep dive into security problems, you can also get a general feel for what is going on with your captured data by reviewing the Expert Info. In the DNS Remoteshell pcap file, we can review the Expert Info in Figure 9.13. Here we see specific Denial of Service (DoS) attempts by constant connection establishment

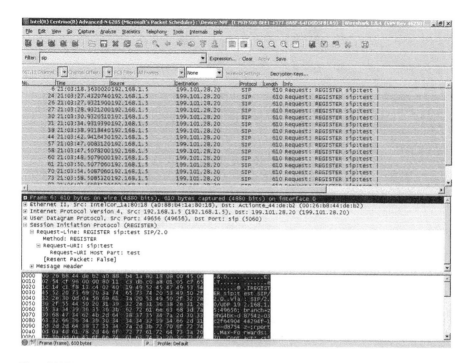

Figure 9.10 Viewing SIP connections in Wireshark.

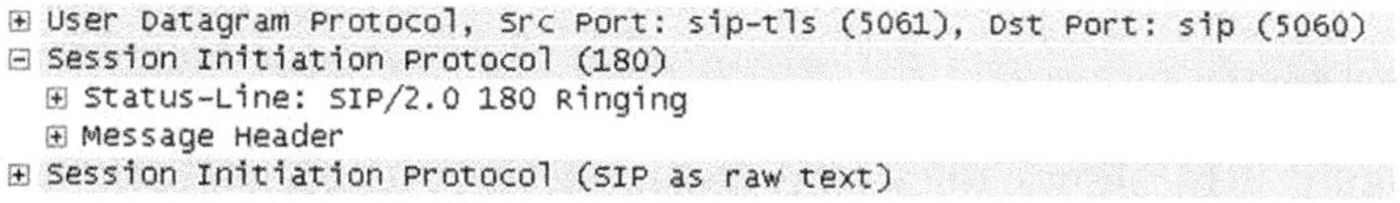

⊞ User Datagram Protocol, Src Port: sip-tls (5061), Dst Port: sip (5060)
⊟ Session Initiation Protocol (180)
　⊞ Status-Line: SIP/2.0 180 Ringing
　⊞ Message Header
⊞ Session Initiation Protocol (SIP as raw text)

Figure 9.11 Viewing SIP in the Detail pane.

requests. This also relates to the TCP handshake sequence we learned about earlier.

By taking a quick look at the Expert, we can see constant SYNs until a RST (reset) takes place.

We can also review the Teardrop pcap file. This is another form of a DoS attack. This type of attack takes place by a host sending "mangled" data (IP fragments) with problematic payload sizes to a destination (target) system. By doing so, they could potentially crash the destination system if it becomes overwhelmed.

Figure 9.12 Reviewing SIP statistics.

Figure 9.14 shows the detail pane where you can see the payload sizes and if you do analysis on multiple attempts at the destination, you could find that the mangled data fragments occur at differing sizes which could potentially be problematic to the target system.

Wireshark can quickly and easily help you identify problems with security on your network. For example, if you wanted to capture cleartext passwords, you can do so with Wireshark. TCP/IP version 4 protocols, such as FTP, Telnet, SNMP, and others send data in cleartext and if captured, the credentials to a system could be read and compromised.

9.6 NETWORK PERFORMANCE ANALYSIS AND OPTIMIZATION

Another problem you may have to contend with (and optimize) is application traffic crippling your WAN connections. Application

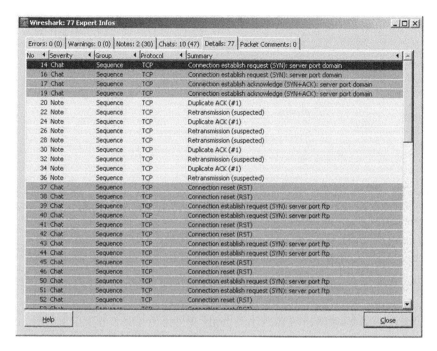

Figure 9.13 Using the expert analysis to find security issues.

```
⊟ User Datagram Protocol, Src Port: 31915 (31915), Dst Port: 20197 (20197)
      Source port: 31915 (31915)
      Destination port: 20197 (20197)
  ⊞ Length: 36 (bogus, payload length 28)
  ⊞ Checksum: 0x0000 (none)
⊞ Data (20 bytes)
```

Figure 9.14 Using the Detail pane to find security issues.

analysis is the hallmark of an experienced technician. As the network or protocol analyst, it is your organization's responsibility to make sure that you know what protocols are being introduced into the network. It is up to you to be able to use a tool-like Wireshark to capture and analyze them to solve problems. You can use Timestamps in the Wireshark capture window Summary pane to analyze response times through time stamp analysis. This will help you rule out latency issues. You can also use Wireshark to find out if bandwidth is an issue.

You can use tools and analyze the bandwidth being used over a WAN link (as an example) to verify that you have enough so data can traverse a network without issues. If you are using a 100 Mbps

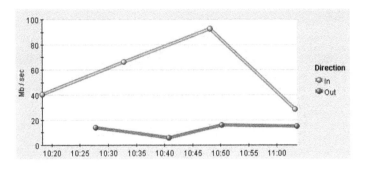

Figure 9.15 Finding network performance issues.

connection and find that you are maxing out the bandwidth, then you can use Wireshark to see if data is retransmitting because of it. Figure 9.15 shows how this solution could be found on your network.

Do not mistake a latency problem with a bandwidth problem. Do not increase your bandwidth because an application responds slowly—the increased bandwidth may not help. Work with your ISP to get statistics on overall bandwidth and utilization so you can see if you are operating at poor levels. Many times, it is simply that the server's response time is poor, the buffers in routing devices or servers are inundated, or a poorly written application will just not function as advertised.

Each suggestion has its own benefits and problems, but a total optimization standpoint, you can use these as ideas to figure out how to make the application work better on your network. Remember, it is not always the network's fault! Some applications were just not made to function well over a WAN link. It is up to you to use your skills and Wireshark to help optimize the traffic that does exist.

●●●

Implement Quality of Service (QoS) on your networking hardware to queue up that application first. QoS will only help if you have a bandwidth issue.

You can also use other tools to help solve problems. In this chapter, we learned about a system having an issue accessing a HTTP-based web page on a web server. You can use tools like HttpWatch as seen in Figure 9.16 to help analyze response time when a client attempts to access a web server.

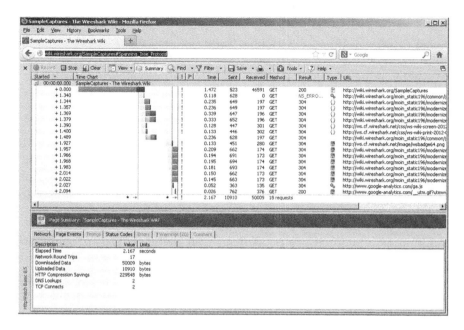

Figure 9.16 Finding application issues.

In this example, we can see how using other tools with Wireshark can aid in helping you find root cause of an issue, or help you rule out what may or may not be impacting the network or systems.

> Beware of compounded issues. Sometimes you may encounter a problem that manifests as a network problem but could be a problematic system, an application problem, or a combination of these problems that when load is added to the systems or network or application access causes a performance problem. Use Wireshark and many of the other tools we covered in this field guide to peel back the layers of the onion and attempt to move towards finding root cause. Typically it makes sense to start the troubleshooting effort at the client (point of problem or complaint) and work your way through the network to the system or systems in which they are trying to use.

Bottlenecks can also be a problem. Choke points from improperly designed networks and systems can cause performance issues. Overwhelmed devices that are undersized to handle the load can cause performance issues. If too much traffic is going through any one source of communication, it may overwhelm the device's ability to process the traffic. This will cause dropped packets, which will require the originating system to resend them, increasing the load on your network. To optimize Ethernet-based networks, you can design your network properly with a high-speed backbone and high-speed desktop switching. Make sure your servers, routers, desktops, or any other device are not the source of the bottleneck.

Unnecessary protocols, which depend on broadcast traffic, can increase the amount of traffic on your network. Also, multicast traffic such as name resolution and switch and bridge updates can consume bandwidth needed for other traffic. To optimize Ethernet, you can do the following:

- Eliminate unneeded protocols from your network hosts (clients, servers, routers, etc.).
- Eliminate unneeded hosts on your network that are not in use and are perhaps sending out keepalives or some other traffic on the wire (make the collision domain smaller).
- Use Switching instead of shared access hubs.
- Implement VLANs if possible to separate broadcast domains or use a router to block broadcast traffic.
- Watch for high percentages of network utilization. It can vary from network to network, but anything over 40% is generally too high on an Ethernet network. If you are on a switched network, then anything over 70% is too high.
- Watch for hardware-related errors. Jabbers or failing NICs often cause long or short frames and Cyclic Redundancy Check (CRC) errors. Correct these problems as they are found.
- Broadcasts and multicasts should be no more than 20% of all network traffic.
- On Ethernet networks there should be no more than 1 CRC error per 1 million bytes of data.

You can also ask specific questions to help you get closer to an answer:

- Is poor network performance affecting one user, several users, or the entire network?
- Is the poor performance centered at a particular location or the entire network?

- When exactly did you start noticing poor performance or has it always been bad?
- Have any recent changes taken place—no matter how large or small?
- Do you have any network documentation or topology maps?

Always try to see if poor network performance is affecting one user, several users, or the entire network. Isolate your problems and nail them down one at a time, if possible.

Always view network documentation and topology maps, if available, to try to find out whether the initial design itself is causing performance issues. You need not use Wireshark immediately to formulate a clue on where the problems lie; detailed topology maps speak for themselves, however, you can run a sample capture to help ascertain a clue or two.

When you are initially analyzing performance on a network, it is important to interview the staff (both users and administrators) to get a solid picture of network health from a "maintenance performed" point of view. Involve vendor support if needed. Ask administrators about changes made to the network recently, find out if things had gotten bad at a specific time, and use the information you gather as part of your analysis. Often changes made to a network result in poor performance, and the staff might be unaware of the cause.

Always involve your ISP in your overall analysis if you cannot verify the connecting links. Ask for service-level agreements (SLAs) if they are available and bandwidth utilization charts if they keep them. This information will help you get a bigger picture of possible performance problems.

9.7 USING WIRESHARK ONLINE

You can always do deeper dives into captured data by simply using Wireshark's ability to link to online documentation. In Figure 9.17, you can see a specific example of how to click and pull up a menu from data in the Detail pane to produce a link where you can pull up the Wireshark Wiki pages to help explain specific data you may or

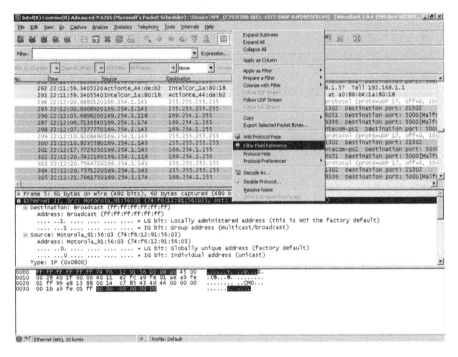

Figure 9.17 Finding online references via Wireshark.

may not understand. This is a great way to help you learn more and dig deeper into the protocols and data you are working with.

9.8 SUMMARY

In this chapter, we covered the specifics of digging deeper. With a deeper look into the data, the systems, and the network, we saw how we could better define and find root cause of problems as well as how to use Wireshark and other enterprise tools to solve issues that occur over WAN links, when using a softphone and to find security problems and so on. In the next and final chapter, we will look at the myriad of ways to handle the data you captured for analysis and safekeeping.

Saving Captures

Wireshark can be used to isolate and troubleshoot network and system problems, and we have flipped open the hood and taken a look into its inner workings. In this field guide, we have learned how to use Wireshark to capture and filter data in hopes that by doing so, we can solve problems. We have learned quite a bit in a short amount of time. In this chapter, we will cover how to save your files, import and export data, and other key information on how to store your captured packets for further analysis.

In this chapter, we will learn how to save captured data. It is not as simple as saving a file; there are many options that you can select, and understanding the options available will help you in making the correct decisions on how and where you want to save your data.

Make sure that when you prepare to save data, you have plenty of disk space available, i.e., a system with the proper resources to handle this task. It is recommended that you also consider encrypting this data if you consider it sensitive. You should also make sure that you follow the practice of ensuring that you limit who can access the data by securing the system or storage device in which it is stored as filtered data can contain secure information such as passwords.

10.1 GETTING STARTED

Once you have completed your analysis, you may want to save and archive your files for future use. This chapter covers file formats, how to use capture files with other protocol analysis systems, how to merge files, and more. In Section 10.2, we review the basics of saving captured data.

When working on a network, a running Wireshark with the intention of capturing and saving data, there are times where you may want to know how you will save it before you even start the capture. In the sections within this chapter, we will cover when that would be applicable. For now, we will cover the basics of saving a capture file once your capture is completed.

10.2 SAVING CAPTURES

Once you are done capturing data, there are many options available to you for controlling the data you wish to store. When you run a capture, all of the data is viewable in the Wireshark capture window. You may want to save all of the captured data or a subset of it. There are options available for both. Before we cover these options, you should consider the following essential guidelines:

1. If you are going to be running captures over a longer period of time, you may wish to break them up into more manageable chunks to store and review from. For most systems, anything more than a 256-megabyte file size is too big.
2. You should consider how you will label your stored files. This way, when you want to access specific portions of saved data, you have a viewable reference by viewing just the file name. For example, if you are capturing data to and from a specific set of IP addresses, you may want to label them in the file name. You should also consider folderizing your saved data for easy reference.
3. Always consider where you will be storing this data (size, security, accessibility, etc).

In Figure 10.1, the Wireshark main page shows options for viewing saved files. In the Open section, you can see the most recently saved files that you can open. They will be colored blue (hyperlink), and by clicking on them, you will open that particular capture. You can also click directly on the Open link denoted by the image of the folder to open the Open Capture File dialog box.

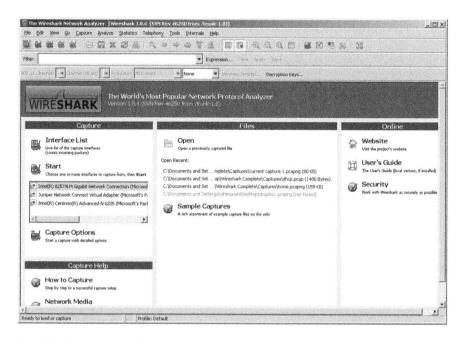

Figure 10.1 Opening capture files.

To save data, simply open Wireshark and run a capture. Stop the capture and go to the Wireshark capture window's menu system. By clicking on File, you will see a drop-down menu of options in which you can save your data. By selecting Save As, you can then name your file and store it in a location of your choice. By clicking on Save, you will be presented with the same options; however, if you already have saved the file, by selecting Save you can update the currently saved file with the newest information, e.g., when you want to continue your capture and collect more packets. This is fairly straightforward. If you want to perhaps save data in groupings of files, you have to go another route.

10.3 SAVING CAPTURES (MULTIPLE FILES)

There may come a time where you want to save a capture in a subset of files. In order to do this, you need to configure Wireshark to handle this task before you start the capture of your data. To do this, you need to first go to the Wireshark launch page, or you can do it from within the Wireshark capture window if you are starting a new capture saving to multiple files. In the Wireshark capture window, you can click on Capture menu option and select Options. On the launch page, you can click on the Capture Options link.

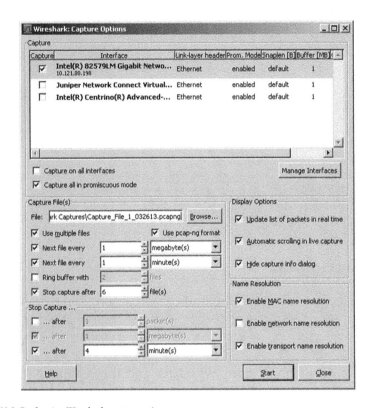

Figure 10.2 Configuring Wireshark capture options.

Once you select either, you will see the Wireshark Capture Options dialog box as shown in Figure 10.2.

Within this dialog box, you see many options you can select and choose from. The relevant area in the dialog box where you will configure the captured data for population into multiple files is in the Capture File(s) section. Here, you can choose the location in which you would like to store your data. Figure 10.3 shows the location of where you would set your capture file when selecting the Browse button.

Once you are done, you can click OK. Then, you can configure options on where you will save the files as well as how to size it, time it, and control it. Once you have selected your relevant options, click Start to begin the capture.

Once the capture has started and run through its routine and stops, you can view these files within the Wireshark capture window by

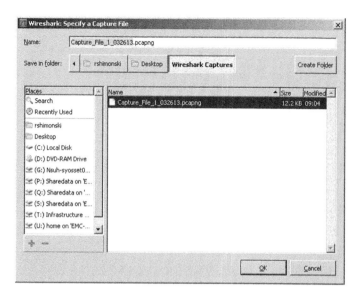

Figure 10.3 Wireshark specific a capture file dialog box.

	Filename	Created	Last Modified	Size
○	Capture_File_1_032613_00001_20130326091456.pcapng	2013.03.26 09:14:56	2013.03.26 09:15:56	139496 Bytes
○	Capture_File_1_032613_00002_20130326091556.pcapng	2013.03.26 09:15:56	2013.03.26 09:16:56	395520 Bytes
○	Capture_File_1_032613_00003_20130326091656.pcapng	2013.03.26 09:16:56	2013.03.26 09:17:56	216056 Bytes
◉	Capture_File_1_032613_00004_20130326091756.pcapng	2013.03.26 09:17:56	2013.03.26 09:18:56	143900 Bytes

... in directory: C:\Documents and Settings\rshimonski\Desktop\Wireshark Captures

Figure 10.4 Wireshark list files dialog box.

clicking on the File menu and selecting File Set. Expand this option to view List Files as shown in Figure 10.4.

To view the same files where they are stored, you can go to the File menu and click Save As and/or simply navigate to the location in which you decided to store the files. As shown in Figure 10.5 you can see how Wireshark chunked out the capture into multiple files.

10.4 SAVING IN OTHER FORMATS

Once you have finished your capture, you can save the capture in many file formats. By going to the File menu and selecting Save As, you can then select the Save as type as shown in Figure 10.6

Figure 10.5 Wireshark saving data in multiple files.

Figure 10.6 Saving files in multiple formats.

There may be times where you would like to save the captured data in the native format of the tool you may be transferring the data to, e.g., if you want to send captured data to another associate helping you troubleshoot, and they use Microsoft Network Monitor, you can choose to save in the native format for that specific tool. You can see the different file extensions in Figure 10.6 from the Save as type menu. Click Save to complete this task.

10.5 IMPORTING AND EXPORTING DATA

When saving data, there may be times where you simply want to save a portion of this data for use. A great example would be when you ran a large capture and had a lot of data in your window that you did not want to save. You could filter out this data and export the relevant data to a new file. You can also import data into a file.

To import data into a file, go to the File menu and select Import from the drop-down menu. You will then open the Wireshark Import from Text dialog box as shown in Figure 10.7.

When using this option, you will need to select a preconfigured text file with the relevant data already configured in the file to import.

To export data, simple click on the File menu again and select from the multiple Export options listed. Depending on where you are in the Wireshark capture window and what data you have captured will then give you the specific options for what you can export; otherwise, the option will be grayed out and unusable.

In Figure 10.8, the option to Export Specified Packets was chosen. This was predetermined from the example provided earlier where we wanted to filter out the data we did not want to use and populate a new file for reference.

You will not be able to use the filter option if you do not choose "displayed" in the export options for Packet Range.

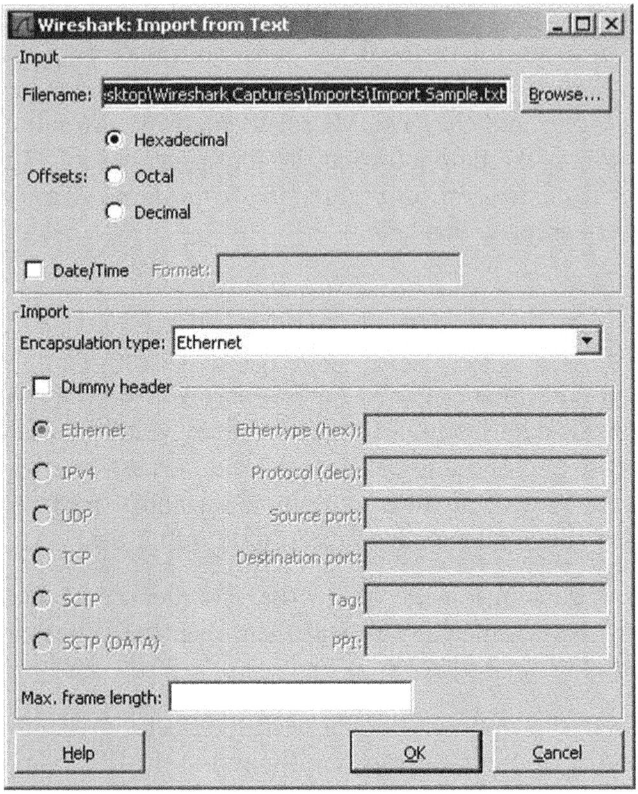

Figure 10.7 Import from text.

10.6 MERGING DATA

Once you have captured multiple files, there may come a time where you want to reassemble the data into one file. To do this, you can choose the merge option. In the File menu, you can select Merge to open the Merge with capture file dialog box as shown in Figure 10.9.

To merge data, you will need to select a file name where you will merge to. You can also configure a Display filter as well as select other options for prepending and appending.

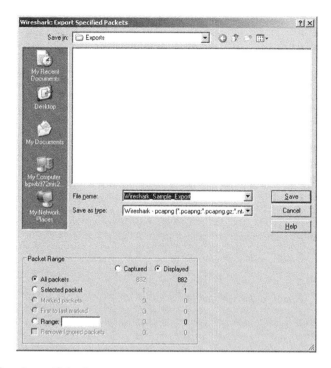

Figure 10.8 Exporting specified packets.

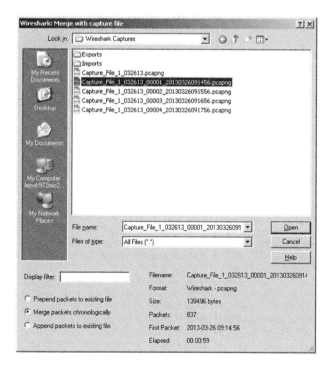

Figure 10.9 Merging capture files.

10.7 SUMMARY

Now you know how to save data to files for storage and future analysis. You can send these files to others to troubleshoot as a team or get help from others.

We have completed the final steps of learning Wireshark in this field guide. This is written in the hope of getting you up to speed quickly in using one of the most common network-based troubleshooting tools used in the industry today. To learn more, visit the websites listed in this book.

Printed and bound by CPI Group (UK) Ltd, Croydon, CR0 4YY

03/10/2024

01040423-0015